CAMBRIDGE GED PROGRAM

EXERCISE BOOK FOR Interpreting Literature and the Arts

CAMBRIDGE ADULT EDUCATION
A Division of Simon & Schuster
Upper Saddle River, New Jersey

NEW REVISED CAMBRIDGE GED PROGRAM

WRITERS
Beverly Ann Chin
Gloria Levine
Karen Wunderman
Stella Sands
Michael Ross
Alan Hines
Donald Gerstein

CONSULTANTS/REVIEWERS
Marjorie Jacobs
Cecily Bodnar
Diane Hardison
Dr. Margaret Tinzmann
Nora Chomitz
Bert C. Honigman
Sylvester Pues

COVER
Art Director: Josée Ungaretta
Cover Design: Marta Wolchuk, Design Five, NYC
Cover Illustration: Min Jae Hong

Copyright © 1994, 1998 by Globe Fearon, Inc. A Simon & Schuster Company. One Lake Street, Upper Saddle River, New Jersey 07458. All rights reserved. No part of this book may be reproduced or transmitted in any form or by any means, electronic, photographic, mechanical, or otherwise, including photocopying, recording, or by any information storage and retrieval system, without permission in writing from the publisher.

The editors have made every effort to trace the ownership of all copyrighted material and express regret in advance for any error or omission. After notification of an oversight, they will include proper notification in future printings.

Printed in the United States of America

3 4 5 6 7 8 9 10 01 00 99

ISBN 0-835-94735-1

CAMBRIDGE ADULT EDUCATION
A Division of Simon & Schuster
Upper Saddle River, New Jersey

Contents

Introduction

This Exercise Book for the Interpreting Literature and the Arts Test can help you prepare for the fourth test of the GED. You can use it along with either the *Cambridge Comprehensive Program for the High School Equivalency Examination* or the *Cambridge Program for the Interpreting Literature and the Arts Test.*

The Three Sections of this Book

This book has three sections: Exercise, Practice, and Simulation. All three sections share a common purpose—to provide you with practice at reading the types of passages and answering the types of questions you will find when you take the GED. All the passages and questions in this book are like those you will find on the actual Interpreting Literature and the Arts Test.

The paragraphs that follow explain what the sections of this book are and tell you how to use them to your best advantage.

The Exercise Section

What Is the Exercise Section? The Exercise section allows you to practice one type of literature at a time. It is made up of passages and questions grouped by the types of literature as they are grouped in Unit II of the *Cambridge Program for the Interpreting Literature and the Arts Test* and Unit VI of the *Cambridge Comprehensive Program.* There are five groups of exercises, one for each of the types of literature covered in Chapters 2 through 6 in either book. For example, for the chapter on nonfiction in the Cambridge Programs, you will find a corresponding group of exercises in this book that are based solely on nonfiction.

How to Use The Exercise Section. After you complete a chapter in either of the Cambridge Programs, you can practice by using the corresponding exercise in this book. This allows you to practice with skills you have just studied in order to reinforce them. If you'd rather, however, you can wait until after you've studied a group of chapters and then complete the related exercises to test several of your literature skills at once. It would probably be best for you to complete the exercises in this book before you work on the corresponding Practice Items in the textbooks.

The Practice Tests

What Are the Practice Tests? This book has two practice tests that are structured like the actual Interpreting Literature and the Arts Test of the GED. The passages and questions on the Practice Tests are *not* grouped according to type. Rather, they vary from passage to passage, just as on the real test. The first test, the Half-length Practice Test, is made up of 23 items—about half as many as make up the actual GED. The second practice test is full-length, the same length as the real test. Both tests give you an opportunity to practice taking a test similar to the GED.

How to Use the Practice Tests. You should take the Practice Tests after you have completed the literature instruction chapters in a Cambridge Program and the Exercises in this book. It would probably be best to take the Practice Tests in this book after you complete the Practice section in either textbook. The Half-length Practice Test should take 33 minutes. The Full-length Practice Test should take 65 minutes, the same amount of time allowed on the actual GED test.

The Simulated Test

What Is the Simulated Test? The Simulated Test is as much like the actual GED test as possible. It has the same number of questions and is just as challenging as the real test. As on the Practice Tests, the type of literature varies from passage to passage. Taking the Simulated Test will help you determine how ready you are to take the real GED test.

How to Use the Simulated Test. You can take the Simulated Test before or after you've taken the Simulated Interpreting Literature and the Arts Test in one of the Cambridge Programs. Take the Simulated Test under the same conditions as you will have when you take the real Interpreting Literature and the Arts Test—work without interruption and do not talk to anyone or consult other materials. You should complete the Simulated Test in 65 minutes, the same amount of time you will have on the actual GED.

Scoring Your Work and Using Your Scores

You will find that the answer key is a very useful study tool. When you complete a section in this book, compare your answers to the correct answers in the answer key. Whether you answer an item correctly or not, you should read through the information that explains each correct answer. Doing this will reinforce your knowledge of literature and develop your test-taking skills. After you check your answers to the items on one of the three tests, you can complete the appropriate Performance Analysis Chart. The charts can help you determine which skills and areas you are strongest in, and direct you to parts of the Cambridge Programs where you can review areas in which you need additional work.

Nonfiction Items

Directions: Choose the one best answer for each question.

Items 1 to 5 are based on the following passage.

WHY IS HOUDINI A MEMORABLE CHARACTER?

There is in this sudden ending to a career which had its heroic aspect something ironic and tragic. It shocks us that Houdini, not much over fifty and at the most interesting point of his career, should thus have fallen a victim to one of the most trivial of his challenges, to a blow by a college student, given under a misapprehension, when he was ill and reading his mail.

Houdini was the son of a rabbi. His parents had come from Budapest, and settled in Appleton, Wisconsin. The father knew no English; they were poor. Houdini (whose real name was Ehrich Weiss) went off at the age of eleven to earn his own living. He had already learned to do tricks from the conjurers in circus side shows, and, while working in a locksmith's shop, had mastered the technique of picking locks: he could already, in fact, open handcuffs. He had from the beginning the magician's vocation. He was by turns a messenger-boy, a necktie-cutter and a Wild Man in a tent of freaks; but his concentration on magic was as fervent and unremitting as Lindbergh's concentration on flying.

Houdini had, thus, in his field, the all-absorbing preoccupation of genius, but he was remarkable also for other qualities, the virtues of his sober, pious and self-respecting German Jewish family, virtues that he managed to preserve through the humiliations and hardships of his early years. Houdini remained all his life, in spite of considerable egotism, the scrupulous, industrious, loyal and generous son of his parents. It was partly this background of family life—his devotion to his wife and his mother is one of his most striking traits—which gave him his solidity and straightness. When, in Yorkshire once, a former hangman who had retired to run a public-house, attempted to bribe the champion, proposing to bet large sums on his ability to tie him up in such a way that he could not escape and then, when Houdini had "thrown" the contest, to divide the winnings with him. Houdini wrote contemptuously in his diary: "Guess he didn't know how I was brought up."

Excerpt from "A Great Magician" from *The Shores of Light* by Edmund Wilson. Copyright © 1953 by Edmund Wilson. Copyright renewed © 1983 by Helen Mirand Wilson. Reprinted by permission of Hill and Wang, a division of Farrar, Straus and Giroux, Inc.

1. According to the author, Houdini was

(1) a greatly overrated magician
(2) a skilled and honest man
(3) a hard-working miser
(4) a proud but selfish artist
(5) an unfaithful husband

2. How had Houdini learned to open handcuffs?

(1) He had watched circus performers do it.
(2) He had read about the technique in a book.
(3) He had worked in a locksmith's shop.
(4) His father had taught him.
(5) A fellow prisoner had taught him.

3. The author indicates that Houdini died as the result of
   (1) a disease
   (2) suicide
   (3) an accident
   (4) old age
   (5) murder

4. How does the author emphasize Houdini's devotion to the art of magic?
   (1) by telling a story about a man from Yorkshire
   (2) by describing the hardships of his childhood
   (3) by revealing that he once worked in a circus
   (4) by comparing him to Lindbergh, a man known for his passion for flying
   (5) by providing information about his death

5. Based on the description of Houdini in lines 29–43, which of the following deeds would he be LEAST likely to do?
   (1) forget his mother's birthday
   (2) make an anonymous gift to a charity
   (3) care for his sick wife
   (4) attend a religious service
   (5) work at two jobs to support his family

Items 6 to 10 are based on the following passage.

HOW WAS THE EMANCIPATION PROCLAMATION A MIXED BLESSING?

...The most distinct thing that I now recall in connection with the scene was that some man who seemed to be a stranger (a United States officer, I presume) made a little speech and then read a rather long paper—the Emancipation Proclamation, I think. After the reading we were told that we were all free, and could go when and where we pleased. My mother, who was standing by my side, leaned over and kissed her children, while tears of joy ran down her cheeks. She explained to us what it all meant, that this was the day for which she had been so long praying, but fearing that she would never live to see.

For some minutes there was great rejoicing, and thanksgiving, and wild scenes of ecstasy. But there was no feeling of bitterness. In fact, there was pity among the slaves for our former owners. The wild rejoicing on the part of the emancipated coloured people lasted but for a brief period, for I noticed that by the time they returned to their cabins there was a change in their feelings.... In a few hours the great questions with which the Anglo-Saxon race had been grappling for centuries had been thrown upon these people to be solved. These were the questions of a home, a living, the rearing of children, education, citizenship, and the establishment and support of churches. Was it any wonder that within a few hours the wild rejoicing ceased and a feeling of deep gloom seemed to pervade the slave quarters? To some it seemed that, now that they were in actual possession of it, freedom was a more serious thing than they had expected to find it. Some of the slaves were seventy or eighty years old; their best days were gone. They had no strength with which to earn a living in a strange place and among strange people, even if they had been sure where to find a new place of abode. To this class the problem seemed especially hard. Besides, deep down in their hearts there was a strange and peculiar attachment to "old Master" and "old Missus," and to their children, which they found it hard to think of breaking off. With these they had spent in some cases nearly a half-century, and it was no light thing to think of parting. Gradually, one by one, stealthily at first, the older slaves began to wander from the slave quarters back to the "big house" to have a whispered conversation with their former owners as to the future.

From *Up From Slavery* by Booker T. Washington

6. Who reads the text of the Emancipation Proclamation to the author and his fellow slaves?

(1) the owner of the plantation
(2) the eldest son of their master
(3) a special courier from President Lincoln
(4) the best educated of the slaves
(5) a stranger

7. Which word best describes the slaves' attitude toward their ex-masters?

(1) indifference
(2) hatred
(3) scorn
(4) compassion
(5) curiosity

8. What is the probable topic of the "whispered conversation" of the older slaves at the "big house" (lines 55–60)?

(1) requests for loans of money with which to start a new life
(2) methods for escaping to freedom
(3) hopes for remaining in the owner's employ
(4) plans for dealing with the departure of the younger slaves
(5) recollections of happier days before the war

9. When the author uses the phrases "old Master" and "old Missus" (line 50), he is using the slaves' terms

(1) to reinforce the idea of a lingering affection
(2) to reinforce the idea of hatred
(3) to suggest that the former owners could not take care of themselves
(4) to emphasize the inhumanity of slavery
(5) to suggest a feeling of betrayal

10. The author tells of the slaves' problem primarily by

(1) writing from a child's point of view
(2) quoting the reactions of a number of slaves
(3) focusing on the reactions of one family of slaves
(4) offering his insights into the events that he describes
(5) imagining the thoughts of the former masters

Items 11 to 16 are based on the following passage.

WHAT DECISIONS DO KAREN'S PARENTS MAKE?

"How are these children going to learn so they can lead useful happy lives?"

Dr. B said, "I wish I knew. Today, only one out of a hundred is receiving necessary treatment and education. And every fifty-three minutes another C.P. is born, to say nothing of the tens of thousands who acquire the condition later in life."

He leaned over and picked up a fresh cigarette and lit it from the one he was smoking. Here at long last we had found a solution—and at the moment of finding it, it was snatched away. Jimmy slapped both his hands sharply on the desk and jumped to his feet.

"I don't believe it. This is America—the land of equal opportunity." His voice was raw. "What a laugh!" He marched over to the window and turned. "It's a sin—a shame. By God, we haven't spent all this time finding the answer to forfeit it. There must be something, some way—"...

"Doctor, why can't *we* learn, why can't *we* learn to do therapy ourselves?"

Dr. B stood up and came over to sit on the edge of the desk in front of Jimmy. "You can," he answered....

The first week-end after our return, we held a family conclave. We discussed our "situation" (having first decided that we would no longer refer to it as a problem). We analyzed the situation in relation to each of us. It was not something that affected just Karen, but all of us. Each of us had emotional attitudes that needed adjusting but there were some general rules of attitude and conduct that applied to all.

1. Karen was a child with a physical handicap but we must not allow this to make us lose sight of the fact that she was a child, first, with all the needs and desires of all children.

2. Many folk with agile limbs are handicapped in the true sense, by a phony set of values, faulty character, etc.

3. Karen should have compassion—but pity, never.

4. There must never be overprotection. Any fears we have must be conquered or concealed. Fear would undermine and destroy.

5. Our efforts were toward this goal: that Karen would one day be a self-respecting, a self-supporting member of society.

To this end we would in the future refer to Karen, not as being *afflicted* with cerebral palsy, but as being *affected* by palsy.

Excerpt from the book, *Karen* by Marie Killilea. Copyright © 1952, 1980. Used by permission of Prentice Hall/A division of Simon & Schuster, Englewood Cliffs, N.J.

11. What is the topic of both conversations in this passage?

(1) the increase in cases of cerebral palsy
(2) helping Karen to become productive and happy
(3) defining family rules of conduct toward Karen
(4) ways of paying for Karen's therapy
(5) Karen's growing depression

12. In what way does the author suggest how frustrated the family feels?

(1) by voicing her own fears about Karen's future
(2) by hinting indirectly at Karen's poor health
(3) by focusing on Jimmy's reaction to the doctor's news
(4) by allowing Karen to speak for herself about her condition
(5) by describing Karen's condition in graphic detail

13. The events in the passage reveal that

(1) all disabled children face a frightening future
(2) Karen's family has reached a turning point in their lives
(3) Jimmy is becoming emotionally unbalanced
(4) Dr. B secretly despises handicapped people
(5) Karen has not yet learned to cope with her disability

14. Which of the following best describes Dr. B?

(1) practical but intense
(2) cheerfully idealistic
(3) despairingly sad
(4) bitter and stern
(5) self-confident and optimistic

15. Which of the following would Karen's family consider to be the greatest handicap?

(1) blindness
(2) deafness
(3) paralysis
(4) hard-heartedness
(5) mental retardation

16. Why does the author refer to the doctor as Dr. B?

(1) to protect the doctor's identity

(2) to show how friendly the family and doctor are

(3) to emphasize how distant the family and doctor are

(4) to suggest that the family doesn't know the doctor's real name

(5) to show a contrast between the doctor and the family

Items 17 to 21 are based on the following passage.

CAN PUBLIC RECOGNITION BE DANGEROUS?

SIRS:–I wish to acknowledge your choice of my novel *Arrowsmith* for the Pulitzer Prize. That prize I must refuse, and my refusal would be meaningless unless I explained the reasons.

All prizes, like all titles, are dangerous. The seekers for prizes tend to labor not for inherent excellence but for alien rewards: They tend to write this, or timorously to avoid writing that, in order to tickle the prejudices of a haphazard committee. And the Pulitzer Prize for novels is peculiarly objectionable because the terms of it have been constantly and grievously misrepresented.

Those terms are that the prize shall be given "for the American novel published during the year which shall best present the wholesome atmosphere of American life, and the highest standard of American manners and manhood." This phrase, if it means anything whatever, would appear to mean that the appraisal of the novels shall be made not according to their actual literary merit but in obedience to whatever code of Good Form may chance to be popular at the moment....

If already the Pulitzer Prize is so important, it is not absurd to suggest that in another generation it may, with the actual terms of the award ignored, become the one thing for which any ambitious novelist will strive; and the administrators of the prize may become a supreme court, a college of cardinals, so rooted and so sacred that to challenge them will be to commit blasphemy. Such is the French Academy, and we have had the spectacle of even an Anatole France intriguing for election.

Only by regularly refusing the Pulitzer Prize can novelists keep such a power from being permanently set up over them.

Between the Pulitzer Prizes, the American Academy of Arts and Letters and its training-school, the National Institute of Arts and Letters, amateur boards of censorship, and the inquisition of earnest literary ladies, every compulsion is put upon writers to become safe, polite, obedient, and sterile. In protest, I declined election to the National Institute of Arts and Letters some years ago, and now I must decline the Pulitzer Prize.

I invite other writers to consider the fact that by accepting the prizes and approval of these vague institutions we are admitting their authority, publicly confirming them as the final judges of literary excellence, and I inquire whether any prize is worth that subservience.

I am, Sirs,

Yours sincerely,

(Signed) SINCLAIR LEWIS

From "Letter to the Pulitzer Prize Committee" by Sinclair Lewis. First appeared in *The New Statesmen* on May 29, 1928.

17. What is the primary reason that the author gives for writing this letter?

(1) to decline his election to the National Institute of Arts and Letters

(2) to speculate about the importance of art in the future

(3) to explain why he is refusing the Pulitzer Prize

(4) to thank the committee for honoring *Arrowsmith*

(5) to urge the committee to redefine their standards for judging novels

18. The author warns the reader against the Pulitzer Prize committee's growing feeling of self-importance by

(1) speaking of laboring for "alien awards" (lines 8-9)

(2) referring to the "code of Good Form" (line 26)

(3) comparing the Pulitzer Prize committee to the French Academy (lines 32-40)

(4) comparing controversial writing to blasphemy (lines 36-37)

(5) referring to the committee as "the final judge" (line 60)

19. The author quotes the terms of the award (lines 16-21) in order to

(1) reveal secret information to the reading public

(2) praise the committee's judgment

(3) appeal to the reader's imagination

(4) illustrate that the awards are not based primarily on literary value

(5) persuade other authors to write letters of protest

20. Which of the following best describes the approach the author uses in this letter?

(1) sarcastic

(2) polite

(3) apologetic

(4) angry

(5) sympathetic

21. If an actor asked Sinclair Lewis for advice on maintaining artistic freedom in movies, which of the following would most likely be Lewis' response, based on his letter?

(1) "Decline to accept an Oscar."

(2) "Work only in 'underground' films."

(3) "Quit the Screen Actors' Guild."

(4) "Look for parts in controversial movies."

(5) "Encourage your producers to give parts to new, unknown actors."

Items 22 to 26 are based on the following passage.

HOW HAS THE AUTHOR BEEN DISCRIMINATED AGAINST?

As a woman who thinks a needle is something you take out splinters with and step on in your bare feet, I have always been annoyed with the inequality of alterations.

Why is it when a man buys a suit, his alterations come free, but when a woman buys an outfit of equal or more value, she pays extra?

I was with my husband a few years ago when he bought a $49.95 suit (with a vest, two contrasting pairs of slacks, a matching tam, and set of dishes). Not only was it a cheap suit (the label said, "Made in Occupied Guadalcanal: Fashion Capital of the World") but it hung on him like an ugly blind date.

"I don't like the way it breaks across the shoulders," he said, twisting before his three-way mirror. "And the sleeves—I like them short enough to count my fingers. Maybe you can reset them."

"No problem," smiled the salesman.

"There's too much slack in the seat and the waistband seems a little loose... maybe a tuck or two."

"Of course," grinned the salesman. "Let me summon a tailor."

The tailor spent thirty-five minutes chalking up my husband's anatomy. The suit looked like a steer being divided for two freezers—all at no charge.

The other day I tried on a dress of comparable value.

"It bags a little in front," I said, looking sideways into the mirror.

"There are operations to correct that, honey," she yawned. "Or we'll alter it for three dollars."

"And the sleeves. They hang so long."

"That'll be two-fifty or you can roll 'em up and keep your elbows bent."

"I don't know," I pondered. "Maybe a knit isn't for me. It clings so."

"Tell you what," she said, "if you want to save two dollars, just block it yourself by stretching it over a chair for a couple of days... or a sofa depending on how loose you want it."

"How much to shorten it?"

"Four dollars," she said, "but it'll be worth it. This dress will look like it's been made for you. Here, let me help you with the zipper."

"How much for helping me with my zipper," I chided.

"I'll throw it in," she said. "I feel sorry for you."

Erma Bombeck, "Discrimination." From "One Size Fits All of What?," in *I Lost Everything in the Post-Natal Depression* by Erma Bombeck, copyright © 1970, 1971, 1972, 1973, by Field Enterprises, Inc., copyright © 1970, 1971, 1972, by The Hearst Corporation. Reprinted by permission of Doubleday & Co., Inc.

22. What is the topic of this passage?

(1) the high price of clothing
(2) the difference between getting alterations in men's and women's clothing
(3) the poor workmanship of imported clothing
(4) the discourtesy of salespeople
(5) the role of women in contemporary society

23. From the comment about needles in lines 1-3, it can be inferred that the author

(1) is accident-prone
(2) suspects that she deserves the treatment she gets
(3) prefers buying clothes to making them herself
(4) approves of home remedies
(5) is writing to readers who generally are poorly educated

24. Why does the author say "it hung on him like an ugly blind date" (lines 16-17)?

(1) to criticize her husband's taste
(2) to add to the humor of the passage
(3) to contrast her husband's clothes with hers
(4) to complain about her date
(5) to urge people to buy American-made clothing

25. What does the author have to do to get her dress altered?

(1) give the clerk a tip
(2) go to another store
(3) just ask politely
(4) complain to the manager
(5) pay for each alteration

26. Which of the following would the author probably be most likely to agree with?

(1) The store has a fair alteration policy.
(2) Women should not be treated differently from men.
(3) The store clerks should both be fired.
(4) Stores shouldn't alter clothing.
(5) The store should charge more for alterations.

Items 27 to 32 are based on the following passage.

WHAT DOES THIS MAN WANT TO KNOW?

Nameless, Tennessee, was a town of maybe ninety people if you pushed it, a dozen houses along the road, a couple of barns, same number of churches, a general merchandise store selling Fire Chief gasoline, and a community center with a lighted volleyball court. Behind the center was an open-roof, rusting metal privy with PAINT ME on the door; in the hollow of a nearby oak lay a full pint of Jack Daniel's Black Label. From the houses, the odor of coal smoke.

Next to a red tobacco barn stood the general merchandise with a poster of Senator Albert Gore, Jr., smiling from the window. I knocked. The door opened partway. A tall, thin man said, "Closed up. For good," and started to shut the door.

"Don't want to buy anything. Just a question for Mr. Thurmond Watts."

The man peered through the slight opening. He looked me over. "What question would that be?"

"If this is Nameless, Tennessee, could he tell me how it got that name?"

The man turned back into the store and called out, "Miss Ginny! Somebody here wants to know how Nameless come to be Nameless."

Miss Ginny edged to the door and looked me and my truck over. Clearly, she didn't approve. She said, "You know as well as I do, Thurmond. Don't keep him on the stoop in the damp to tell him." Miss Ginny, I found out, was Mrs. Virginia Watts, Thurmond's wife.

I stepped in and they both began telling the story, adding a detail here, the other correcting a fact there, both smiling at the foolishness of it all. It seems the hilltop settlement went for years without a name. Then one day the Post Office Department told the people if they wanted mail up on the mountain they would have to give the place a name you could properly address a letter to. The community met; there were only a handful, but they commenced debating. Some wanted patriotic names, some names from nature, one man recommended in all seriousness his own name. They couldn't agree, and they ran out of names to argue about. Finally, a fellow tired of the talk; he didn't like the mail he received anyway. "Forget the durn Post Office," he said. "This here's a nameless place if I ever seen one, so leave it be." And that's just what they did.

Watts pointed out the window. "We used to have signs on the road, but the Halloween boys keep tearin' them down."

"You think Nameless is a funny name," Miss Ginny said. "I see it plain in your eyes. Well, you take yourself up north a piece to Difficult or Defeated or Shake Rag. Now them are silly names."

Excerpt from *Blue Highways* by William Least Heat Moon
Copyright © 1982 by William Least Heat Moon. By permission of Little, Brown and Company

27. Which of the following best describes Nameless, Tennessee?

(1) a busy city
(2) the state capital
(3) a small town
(4) the highest mountain in the state
(5) an important Post Office

28. Who answers the narrator's questions?

(1) Senator Albert Gore, Jr.
(2) Thurmond Watts and his wife
(3) the founder of Nameless
(4) the town historian
(5) no one

29. Why did the narrator have to ask if this was the town of Nameless?

(1) He couldn't find it on the map.
(2) The Halloween boys had torn down the road signs.
(3) He couldn't read the road signs.
(4) He thought he was lost.
(5) No one wanted to tell him the town's name.

30. Why did the townspeople finally agree on the name?

(1) They thought it had a nice sound.
(2) The Post Office had suggested the name.
(3) They wanted a silly name.
(4) They couldn't agree on anything else.
(5) They thought it sounded patriotic.

31. From the way the story is told, it is likely that

(1) the couple has told it many times
(2) the couple is making it up as they go along
(3) the couple is reading it from a book
(4) the couple never thought much about it before
(5) the couple thinks the story is boring

32. Which of the following is probably true of Difficult, Defeated, and Shake Rag?

(1) They are ghost towns.
(2) They got their names in unusual ways.
(3) Their general merchandise stores are closed.
(4) They aren't worth visiting.
(5) The Post Office won't deliver mail there.

Answers are on pages 84-86

Fiction Items

Directions: Choose the one best answer for each question.

Items 1 to 5 are based on the following passage.

DOES THE MONKEY'S PAW REALLY HAVE MAGIC POWERS?

I'd like to go to India myself," said the old man, "just to look round a bit, you know."

"Better where you are," said the sergeant-major, shaking his head. He put down the empty glass and, sighing softly, shook it again.

"I should like to see those temples and fakirs and jugglers," said the old man. "What was that you started telling me the other day about a monkey's paw or something, Morris?"

"Nothing," said the soldier hastily. "Leastways, nothing worth hearing."

"Monkey's paw?" said Mrs. White curiously.

"Well, it's just a bit of what you might call magic, perhaps," said the sergeant-major offhandedly.

His three listeners leaned forward eagerly. The visitor absentmindedly put his empty glass to his lips and then set it down again. His host filled it for him.

"To look at," said the sergeant-major, fumbling in his pocket, "it's just an ordinary little paw, dried to a mummy."

He took something out of his pocket and proffered it. Mrs. White drew back with a grimace, but her son, taking it, examined it curiously.

"And what is there special about it?" inquired Mr. White, as he took it from his son and, having examined it, placed it upon the table.

"It had a spell put on it by an old fakir," said the sergeant-major, "a very holy man. He wanted to show that fate ruled people's lives, and that those who interfered with it did so to their sorrow. He put a spell on it so that three separate men could each have three wishes from it."

His manner was so impressive that his hearers were conscious that their light laughter jarred somewhat.

"Well, why don't you have three, sir?" said Herbert White cleverly.

The soldier regarded him in the way that middle age is wont to regard presumptuous youth. "I have," he said quietly, and his blotchy face whitened.

"And did you really have the three wishes granted?" asked Mrs. White.

"I did," said the sergeant-major, and his glass tapped against his strong teeth.

"And has anybody else wished?" inquired the old lady.

"The first man had his three wishes, yes," was the reply. "I don't know what the first two were, but the third was for death. That's how I got the paw."

His tones were so grave that a hush fell upon the group.

From "The Monkey's Paw" by W. W. Jacobs.

1. On which topic did the conversation in this passage probably begin?

(1) the Whites' vacation in India
(2) the sergeant-major's experiences in India
(3) the beauty of ancient Indian temples
(4) the nature of magic
(5) the amusing antics of monkeys

2. When the old man raises the subject of the monkey's paw (line 10-12), the sergeant-major
   (1) bows his head and crosses himself
   (2) gets a faraway look in his eye
   (3) turns pale
   (4) tries to change the subject
   (5) laughs

3. What is special about the monkey paw?
   (1) It is owned by a military man.
   (2) It can give its owner three wishes.
   (3) It fits easily in a pocket.
   (4) It makes its owner feel middle-aged.
   (5) It is holy.

4. What do details in the passage suggest about the sergeant-major?
   (1) He would like to know more about the monkey's paw.
   (2) He is amused by the legend of the monkey's paw.
   (3) He fears the monkey's paw.
   (4) He doesn't believe that the monkey's paw has any power.
   (5) He murdered to get the monkey's paw.

5. How did the audience finally react to the sergeant-major's tale?
   (1) with laughter
   (2) with disbelief
   (3) with clever questions
   (4) with silence
   (5) with tears

6. Which of the following words best describes the atmosphere that the author has created in this passage?
   (1) light
   (2) suspenseful
   (3) humorous
   (4) hopeful
   (5) bleak

Items 7 to 12 are based on the following passage.

WHAT DOES THE BOY LEARN FROM MRS. JONES?

"Was I bothering you when I turned that corner?" asked the woman.

"No'm."

"But you put yourself in contact with *me,*" said the woman. "If you think that that contact is going to last awhile, you got another thought coming. When I get through with you, sir, you are going to remember Mrs. Luella Bates Washington Jones."...

The water dripping from his face, the boy looked at her. There was a long pause. A very long pause. After he had dried his face and not knowing what else to do dried it again, the boy turned around, wondering what next. The door was open. He could make a dash for it down the hall. He could run, run, run, run, *run!*

The woman was sitting on the daybed. After a while she said, "I were young once and I wanted things I could not get."

There was another long pause. The boys' mouth opened. Then he frowned, but not knowing he frowned.

The woman said, "Um-hum! You thought I was going to say *but*, didn't you? You thought I was going to say, *but I didn't snatch people's pocketbooks*. Well, I wasn't going to say that." Pause. Silence. "I have done things, too, which I would not tell you, son—neither tell God, if he didn't already know. So you set down while I fix us something to eat. You might run that comb through your hair so you will look presentable."...

When they were finished eating she got up and said, "Now, here, take this ten dollars and buy yourself some blue suede shoes. And next time, do not make the mistake of latching on to *my* pocketbook *nor anybody else's*—because shoes come by devilish like that will burn your feet. I got to get my rest now. But I wish you would behave yourself, son, from here on in."

She led him down the hall to the front door and opened it. "Good night! Behave yourself, boy!" she said, looking out into the street.

The boy wanted to say something else other than, "Thank you, m'am," to Mrs. Luella Bates Washington Jones, but he couldn't do so as he turned at the barren stoop and looked back at the large woman in the door. He barely managed to say, "Thank you," before she shut the door. And he never saw her again.

"Thank You, Ma'am" by Langston Hughes from the *Langston Hughes Reader.* Reprinted by permission of Harold Ober Assoc. Copyright © 1958 by Langston Hughes. Copyright renewed 1986 by George Houston Bass.

7. Why did the boy try to snatch Mrs. Jones's pocketbook?

(1) His friends had dared him to do it.
(2) He wanted to prove that he was an adult.
(3) He wanted money to buy blue suede shoes.
(4) He had seen that Mrs. Jones had a lot of money.
(5) Mrs. Jones had laughed at him in public.

8. The statement "He could run, run, run, run, run!" (lines 18–19) is intended

(1) to reveal the boy's fantasies about blue suede shoes
(2) to predict the outcome of the story
(3) to dramatize the boy's desire to escape
(4) to illustrate the boy's love for adventure
(5) to contrast the boy's youth with Mrs. Jones's age

9. What does Mrs. Jones give the boy?

(1) a bath and a meal
(2) a bath and carfare
(3) a meal and a Bible
(4) a meal and some money
(5) a comb and a pair of shoes

10. Which of the following words best describes Mrs. Jones's feeling toward the young thief by the end of the passage?

(1) grief
(2) sympathy
(3) curiosity
(4) amusement
(5) outrage

11. What does the author intend to suggest by inserting "Pause. Silence." (lines 30–31) in the woman's speech?

(1) The woman is afraid of talking to the boy.
(2) The woman is too angry to speak.
(3) The woman is carefully considering what to say next.
(4) The woman is feeling too sad to speak.
(5) The woman wishes the boy would say something.

12. If the boy listens to Mrs. Jones's advice, what will he probably do in the future?

(1) think carefully before stealing again
(2) steal only to put food on his family's table
(3) become a preacher
(4) return to Mrs. Jones whenever he needs advice
(5) devote his life to helping disadvantaged children

Items 13 to 16 are based on the following passage.

WHY IS RICARDO ANGRY?

"Look," said the photographer, packing his plates swiftly. "We're going. Thanks for nothing."

"Before you go, you must see what I am getting at," said Ricardo. "I am not a mean man. But I *can* be a very angry man. Do I look like a cardboard cutout?"

"Nobody said anybody looked like anything." The photographer hefted his case and started off.

"There is a photographer two blocks over," said Ricardo, pacing him. "They have cutouts. You stand in front of them. It says GRAND HOTEL. They take a picture of you and it looks like you are in the Grand Hotel. Do you see what I mean? My alley is my alley, my life is my life, my son is my son. My son is not cardboard! I saw you putting my son against the wall, so, and thus, in the background. What do you call it—for the correct air? To make the whole attractive, and the lovely lady in front of him?"

"It's getting late," said the photographer, sweating. The model trotted along on the other side of him.

"We are poor people," said Ricardo. "Our doors peel paint, our walls are chipped and cracked, our gutters fume in the street, the alleys are all cobbles. But it fills me with a terrible rage when I see you make over these things as if I had *planned* it this way, as if I had years ago induced the wall to crack. Did you think I knew you were coming and aged the paint? Or that I knew you were coming and put my boy in his dirtiest clothes? We are *not* a studio! We are people and must be given attention as people. Have I made it clear?"

Excerpt from *Sun and Shadow* by Ray Bradbury.
Reprinted by permission of Don Congdon Associates, Inc.
© 1953 by Ray Bradbury; renewed 1981 by Ray Bradbury.

13. How does Ricardo ask to be treated?

(1) as a child
(2) as a peasant
(3) as a king
(4) as a rich man
(5) as a person

14. The passage suggests that Ricardo is

(1) proud
(2) unreasonable
(3) brilliant
(4) jealous
(5) lazy

15. Which is the most likely reason that the author had Ricardo contrast his son with cardboard cutouts?

(1) because cutouts are lifeless objects
(2) because the author believes photographers are like cutouts
(3) because the author sees the son's life being wasted
(4) because the author wants to promote the use of cutouts
(5) because cutouts represent what Ricardo doesn't have

16. If the photographer gave Ricardo's son $20, which of the following actions would Ricardo be most likely to take?

(1) He would ask his son to try to get more money.
(2) He would make his son return the money.
(3) He would praise his son for doing a good job.
(4) He would use the money to repair his house.
(5) He would use the money to buy himself some books.

Items 17 to 21 are based on the following passage.

DO THE MEMBERS OF THIS FAMILY GET ALONG WELL?

The grandmother didn't want to go to Florida. She wanted to visit some of her connections in east Tennessee and she was seizing at every chance to change Bailey's mind. Bailey was the son she lived with, her only boy. He was sitting on the edge of his chair at the table, bent over the orange sports section of the *Journal.* "Now look here, Bailey," she said, "see here, read this," and she stood with one hand on her thin hip and the other rattling the newpaper at his bald head. "Here this fellow that calls himself The Misfit is aloose from the Federal Pen and headed toward Florida and you read here what it says he did to these people. Just you read it. I wouldn't take my children in any direction with a criminal like that aloose in it. I couldn't answer to my conscience if I did."

Bailey didn't look up from his reading so she wheeled around then and faced the children's mother, a young woman in slacks, whose face was as broad and innocent as a cabbage and was tied around with a green head-kerchief that had two points on the top like rabbit's ears. She was sitting on the sofa, feeding the baby his apricots out of a jar. "The children have been to Florida before," the old lady said. "You all ought to take them somewhere else for a change so they would see different parts of the world and be broad. They never have been to east Tennessee."

The children's mother didn't seem to hear her but the eight-year-old boy, John Wesley, a stocky child with glasses, said, "If you don't want to go to Florida, why dontcha stay at home?" He and the little girl, June Star, were reading the funny papers on the floor.

"She wouldn't stay at home to be queen for a day," June Star said without raising her yellow head.

"Yes and what would you do if this fellow, The Misfit, caught you?" the grandmother asked.

"I'd smack his face," John Wesley said.

"She wouldn't stay at home for a million bucks," June Star said. "Afraid she'd miss something. She has to go everywhere we go."

"All right, Miss," the grandmother said. "Just remember that the next time you want me to curl your hair."

June Star said her hair was naturally curly.

Reprinted from *A Good Man Is Hard To Find* by Flannery O'Connor by permission of Harcourt Brace Jovanovich, Inc. Copyright 1953 by Flannery O'Connor; renewed 1981 by Mrs. Regina O'Connor.

17. Which of the following does the grandmother not give as a reason for changing the family's vacation plans?

(1) There is a dangerous criminal loose in Florida.

(2) She does not feel strong enough to travel.

(3) She would prefer to visit Tennessee.

(4) The children have already visited Florida.

(5) The children should broaden their horizons.

18. How many children are in the family?

(1) none

(2) one

(3) two

(4) three

(5) four

19. Which of the following best characterizes John Wesley and June Star?

(1) thoughtful

(2) imaginative

(3) well-behaved

(4) enthusiastic

(5) undisciplined

20. The passage suggests that Bailey and his wife generally

(1) respect the grandmother
(2) fear the grandmother
(3) disregard the grandmother
(4) adore the grandmother
(5) make an unnecessary fuss over the grandmother

21. The author's comparison of the mother's face to a cabbage (lines 24-25) stress that the woman

(1) lacks personality
(2) is sickly
(3) is stirred
(4) is ugly
(5) has wrinkles

Items 23 to 26 are based on the following passage.

WHAT SHATTERS THE SPEAKER'S WORLD?

"Twenty-two years, Maybelle, 22 years," he was saying, "and I got nothing for you, nothing, nothing."

"It's all right, honey you'll get something. Everybody out of work now, you know that."

"It ain't right. Ain't no man ought to eat his woman's food year in and year out, and see his children running wild. Ain't nothing right about that."

"Honey, you took good care of us when you had it. Ain't nobody got nothing nowadays."

"I ain't talking about nobody else, I'm talking about *me*. God knows I try." My mother said something I could not hear, and my father cried out louder, "What must a man do, tell me that?"

"Look, we ain't starving. I git paid every week, and Mrs. Ellis is real nice about giving me things. She gonna let me have Mr. Ellis' old coat for you this winter—"

"God damn Mr. Ellis' coat! And god damn his money! You think I want white folks' leavings? God damn, Maybelle"—and suddenly he sobbed, loudly and painfully, and cried helplessly and hopelessly in the dark night. I had never heard a man cry before. I did not know men ever cried. I covered my ears with my hands but could not cut off the sound of my father's harsh, painful, despairing sobs.

My father was a strong man who would whisk a child upon his shoulders and go singing through the house. My father whittled toys for us and laughed so loud that the great oak seemed to laugh with him, and taught us how to fish and hunt rabbits. How could it be that my father was crying? But the sobs went on, unstifled, finally quieting until I could hear my mother's voice, deep and rich, humming softly as she used to hum to a frightened child.

The world had lost its boundary lines. My mother, who was small and soft, was now the strength of the family; my father who was the rock on which the family had been built, was sobbing like the tiniest child. Everything was suddenly out of tune, like a broken accordian. Where did I fit into this crazy picture? I do not now remember my thoughts, only a feeling of great bewilderment and fear.

Excerpt from "Marigolds" by Eugenia Collier. Copyright ©1969 by Johnson Publishing Company, Inc. Reprinted by permission of the author and *Negro Digest*.

22. Why is the speaker's father so upset?

(1) He hates Mr. Ellis.
(2) He does not have a job.
(3) He is starving.
(4) He does not love Maybelle anymore.
(5) He has had a bad day's hunting.

23. Maybelle's statement "I git paid every week, and Mrs. Ellis is real nice about giving me things" (lines 19–21) indicates that she is the woman's

(1) friend
(2) social worker
(3) employee
(4) neighbor
(5) mother

24. Which of the following kinds of behavior would the speaker have expected of her father before this episode?

(1) applying for food stamps
(2) getting his wardrobe at the Salvation Army
(3) making a kite for the children
(4) beating Maybelle
(5) beating the children

25. By comparing the family's situation to a broken accordian (lines 51-52), the author stresses the speaker's

(1) feeling of confusion
(2) musical talent
(3) growing anger
(4) sense of resentment
(5) physical handicap

26. Why does the speaker worry about her place in the family?

(1) It seems that she will have to find a job, too.
(2) She believes that they will all starve.
(3) She believes that her father will leave them.
(4) She has seen her parent's roles change.
(5) Her father has gone singing through the house.

Items 27 to 32 are based on the following passage.

WHY IS THIS MAN KIND TO HIS ENEMY?

After eight he stopped for a while to look at the sky through the window, and he saw two pensive buzzards [large hawks that eat dead animals] who were drying themselves in the sun on the ridgepole [a horizontal piece of wood along the top of a roof] of the house next door. He went on working with the idea that before lunch it would rain again. The shrill voice of his eleven-year-old son interrupted his concentration.

"Papá."

"What?"

"The Mayor wants to know if you'll pull his tooth."

"Tell him I'm not here."

He was polishing a gold tooth. He held it at arm's length, and examined it with his eyes half closed. His son shouted again from the little waiting room.

"He says you are, too, because he can hear you."

The dentist kept examining the tooth. Only when he had put it on the table with the finished work did he say:

"So much the better."

He operated the drill again. He took several pieces of a bridge out of a cardboard box where he kept the things he still had to do and began to polish the gold.

"Papá."

"What?"

He still hadn't changed his expression.

"He says if you don't take out his tooth, he'll shoot you."

Without hurrying, with an extremely tranquil movement, he stopped pedaling the drill, pushed it away from the chair, and pulled the lower drawer of the table all the way out. There was a revolver. "O.K.," he said. "Tell him to come and shoot me."

He rolled the chair over opposite the door, his hand resting on the edge of the drawer. The Mayor appeared at the door. He had shaved the left side of his face, but the other side, swollen and in pain, had a five-day-old beard. The dentist saw many nights of desperation in his dull eyes. He closed the drawer with his fingertips and said softly:

"Sit down."

"Good morning," said the Mayor.

"Morning," said the dentist.

While the instruments were boiling, the Mayor leaned his skull on the headrest of the chair and felt better. His breath was icy. It was a poor office: an old wooden chair, the pedal drill, a glass case with ceramic bottles. Opposite the chair was a window with a shoulder-high cloth curtain. When he felt the dentist approach, the Mayor braced his heels and opened his mouth.

Aurelio Escovar turned his head toward the light. After inspecting the infected tooth, he closed the Mayor's jaw with a cautious pressure of his fingers.

"It has to be without anesthesia [painkiller]," he said.

"Why?"

"Because you have an abscess [a swollen, infected area of the body]."

The Mayor looked him in the eye. "All right," he said, and tried to smile. The dentist did not return the smile. He brought the basin of sterilized instruments to the worktable and took them out of the water with a pair of cold tweezers, still without hurrying. Then he pushed the spittoon with the tip of his shoe, and went to wash his hands in the washbasin. He did all this without looking at the Mayor. But the Mayor didn't take his eyes off him.

It was a lower wisdom tooth. The dentist spread his feet and grasped the tooth with the hot forceps. The Mayor seized the arms of the chair, braced his feet with all his strength, and felt an icy void in his kidneys, but didn't make a sound. The dentist moved only his wrist. Without rancor, rather with a bitter tenderness, he said:

"Now you'll pay for our twenty dead men."

The Mayor felt the crunch of bones in his jaw, and his eyes filled with tears. But he didn't breathe until he felt the tooth come out. Then he saw it through his tears. It seemed so foreign to his pain that he failed to understand his torture of the five previous nights.

Bent over the spittoon, sweating, panting, he unbuttoned his tunic and reached for the handkerchief in his pants pocket. The dentist gave him a clean cloth.

"Dry your tears," he said.

The Mayor did. He was trembling. While the dentist washed his hands, he saw the crumbling ceiling and a dusty spider web with spider's eggs and dead insects. The dentist returned, drying his hands. "Go to bed," he said, "and gargle with salt water." The Mayor stood up, said goodbye with a casual military salute, and walked toward the door, stretching his legs, without buttoning up his tunic.

"Send the bill," he said.

"To you or the town?"

The Mayor didn't look at him. He closed the door and said through the screen:

"It's the same damn thing."

Excerpt from "One of These Days" in *Collected Stories* by Gabriel García Márquez. Copyright © 1984 by the author. Reprinted by permission of Harper & Row, Publishers.

27. The setting of the passage is most likely

(1) a city neighborhood
(2) a small town in the mountains
(3) an island community
(4) a poor rural area
(5) a settlement on a river

28. When the dentist begins work on the tooth in lines 75-86, the mayor's attitude toward the dentist seems to be mainly one of

(1) anger
(2) confidence
(3) suspicion
(4) hope
(5) despair

29. Why does the dentist say "Now you'll pay for our twenty dead men" (lines 96-97)?

(1) The mayor has killed twenty dentists in this small town.
(2) The mayor and the dentist are political leaders of two different countries.
(3) The mayor has killed twenty of the dentist's children.
(4) The dentist thinks the mayor deserves to die twenty times.
(5) The mayor has killed twenty political comrades of the dentist.

30. If a mugger who was robbing the dentist was shot right in front of him by a policeman, the dentist probably would

(1) run away to escape the danger of the situation

(2) run away to keep from getting involved with the authorities

(3) refuse to press charges against the mugger

(4) give the mugger medical aid

(5) tell the policeman he should never use violence against criminals

31. What is the meaning of the last line of the passage?

(1) The mayor's medical bills are covered by health insurance.

(2) The dentist will not be paid for his work.

(3) The mayor completely controls the town government.

(4) The mayor will deny he came to the dentist.

(5) The dentist eventually will kill the mayor.

32. Which of the following best states the theme of the excerpt?

(1) People with kind instincts cannot kill dictators.

(2) Dictators are as sympathetic as anyone else when they suffer

(3) Dictators can be reformed if they are treated kindly.

(4) Dictatorships gradually wither away on their own.

(5) When any government is failing, the people should help it regain its power.

Answers are on pages 86-88.

Drama Items

Directions: Choose the one best answer for each question.

Items 1 to 5 are based on the following passage.

WHY IS CHRIS SO ANGRY AT KELLER?

CHRIS: I want to know what you did, now what did you do? You had a hundred and twenty cracked engine-heads, now what did you do?

KELLER: If you're going to hang me then I...

CHRIS: I'm listening. God Almighty, I'm listening!

KELLER: *(Their movements now are those of subtle pursuit and escape. Keller keeps a step out of Chris' range as he talks.)*: You're a boy, what could I do! I'm in business, a man is in business; a hundred and twenty cracked, you're out of business; you got a process the process don't work, you're out of business; you don't know how to operate, your stuff is no good; they close you up, they tear up your contracts, what the hell's it to them? You lay forty years into a business and they knock you out in five minutes, what could I do, let them take forty years, let them take my life away? *(His voice cracking.)* I never thought they'd install them. I swear to God. I thought they'd stop 'em before anybody took off.

CHRIS: Then why'd you ship them out?

KELLER: By the time they could spot them I thought I'd have the process going again, and I could show them they needed me and they'd let it go by. But weeks passed and I got no kick-back, so I was going to tell them.

CHRIS: Then why didn't you tell them?

KELLER: It was too late. The paper, it was all over the front page, twenty-one went down, it was too late. They came with handcuffs into the shop, what could I do? *(He sits on bench.)* Chris...Chris, I did it for you, it was a chance and I took it for you. I'm sixty-one years old, when would I have another chance to make something for you? Sixty-one years old you don't get another chance, do ya?

CHRIS: You even knew they wouldn't hold up in the air.

KELLER: I didn't say that....

CHRIS: But you were going to warn them not to use them....

KELLER: But that don't mean....

CHRIS: It means you knew they'd crash.

KELLER: It don't mean that.

CHRIS: Then you *thought* they'd crash.

KELLER: I was afraid maybe....

CHRIS: You were afraid maybe! God in heaven, what kind of a man are you? Kids were hanging in the air by those heads. You knew that!

KELLER: For you, a business for you!

Excerpt from *All My Sons* by Arthur Miller. Copyright © 1947, 1957 by the author. From *Arthur Miller's Collected Plays.* Reprinted by permission of Viking Penguin, a division of Penguin Books USA, Inc.

1. What was wrong with the engine-heads?

(1) They were old.
(2) They were small.
(3) They were clogged.
(4) They were cracked.
(5) They were rusty.

2. The information in the passage suggests that the engine-heads were used in
   (1) cars
   (2) airplanes
   (3) tanks
   (4) ships
   (5) trucks

3. Why does Keller say he sold the defective engine-heads?
   (1) to clear out his inventory
   (2) to save the business for Chris
   (3) to repay a loan
   (4) to take advantage of the best business deal he had ever received
   (5) to keep ahead of a business rival

4. According to the passage, which of the following would Chris probably find the most important?
   (1) making lots of money
   (2) being friendly to other people
   (3) building up your own business
   (4) being charitable to the needy
   (5) maintaining your integrity

5. Which of the following words best describes Keller's tone of voice?
   (1) angry
   (2) sarcastic
   (3) pleading
   (4) bashful
   (5) warm

Items 6 to 11 are based on the following passage.

WHO WINS THIS ARGUMENT?

ARTHUR: I'm not going to be a part of this thing. You can call it cold feet, call it anything you like. *(Phyllis studies him.)*

PHYLLIS *(becoming very grim, moving closer to him.)*: Listen to me, Artie. Listen to me good. I didn't think you needed to hear this before. But you're going to hear it now. We're going out there. Do you want to know why? Because we're not going to be next!

ARTHUR: *(jumping up, slamming down paper.)*: You're out of your mind!

PHYLLIS *(vehemently)*: Sure, I am! I'm out of my mind all right. Talk about being afraid—you don't know *when* to be afraid! *(Moves over in front of sofa.)* I'm crazy with fear because I don't want to be different. I don't want my neighbors looking at us and wondering why we didn't go with them—why we're not like them.

ARTHUR: *(amazed)*: Phyllis—you're making this up! They won't think that!

PHYLLIS *(coming back to him.)*: They *will* think that! We'll be the only ones, the odd ones who wanted to let an ex-convict live with us. They'll look the other way when we walk the streets. They'll freeze up—and when people stop speaking they get nasty—and all of a sudden we won't have any neighbors. *(Pulls him to window.)* We'll be like them! *(Pushes aside drapes. Arthur stands looking at her, and it begins to sink in. She knows it and goes after him.)* We can't be different! We can't afford it! We live on the good will of these people. Your business is in this town. Your neighbors buy us the bread we eat! Do you want them to stop?

ARTHUR: I don't know. . .*(A pleading tone.)* Phyllis—I don't know what to think—if I can go out there.

PHYLLIS *(as Arthur moves slowly.)*: You can! You've got to, or we're finished here. *(Arthur stares at her, not knowing what to say next. She has just about won, and knows it. She moves to him.)* You have a home—a family—a position. Is it so much—my asking you not to throw them away?

ARTHUR: All right. You can stop talking about it. For heaven's sake, no more! *(Moves abruptly toward archway.)*

Excerpt from *Thunder On Sycamore Street* by Reginald Rose. Copyright © 1958 by the author. Reprinted by permission of International Creative Management, Inc.

6. Where does this scene take place?

(1) in Phyllis and Arthur's home
(2) in Phyllis's office
(3) in Arthur's office
(4) at a parole office
(5) on the street in front of their house

7. What is Arthur's profession?

(1) a doctor
(2) a businessman
(3) a writer
(4) a lawyer
(5) a teacher

8. The information in the passage implies that the neighbors

(1) want to be different from one another
(2) don't want an ex-convict living among them
(3) don't like Arthur and Phyllis
(4) want to stop Arthur from making a living
(5) support what Arthur and Phyllis are doing

9. The stage directions in this passage are used

(1) to dramatize Phyllis' inner conflict
(2) to reveal what has happened in the previous scene
(3) to describe what Arthur and Phyllis look like
(4) to show how Arthur reacts to Phyllis's argument
(5) to emphasize the strength of the neighbors' influence

10. Phyllis might be expected to do all of the following EXCEPT

(1) read a bestseller
(2) drive a well-known make of car
(3) buy an experimental painting
(4) live in a traditional house
(5) get her hair cut in a popular style

11. The author uses dashes throughout this passage to show that the actors are supposed to

(1) speak more quickly
(2) pause between phrases
(3) speak loudly
(4) breathe heavily
(5) take a break

Items 12 to 14 are based on the following passage.

WHAT IS THE TOPIC OF THIS COVERSATION?

JENNIE: ... You're a very interesting telephone person, Mr. Schneider ... However, I have literally just walked in the door and I haven't eaten since breakfast ... It was really nice talking to you—Goodbye. *(She hangs up. Stays while he hurriedly dials. Her phone rings, she picks it up.)* ... As you were saying...?

GEORGE: Listen, uh, can I be practical for a second?

JENNIE: For a second... yes.

GEORGE: They're not going to let up, you know.

JENNIE: Who?

GEORGE: The pushers. Leo and Faye. They will persist and push and prod and leave telephone numbers under books until eventually we have that inevitable date.

JENNIE: Nothing is inevitable. Dates are man-made.

GEORGE: Whatever... The point is, I assume you have an active career... I'm a very busy man who needs quiet and a few distractions... So let me propose, in the interest of moving on with our lives, that we get this meeting over with just as soon as possible.

JENNIE: ... Surely you jest.

GEORGE: I'm not asking for a date. Blind dates are the nation's third leading cause of skin rash.

JENNIE: Then what are you suggesting?

GEORGE: Just hear me out. What if we were to meet for just five minutes? We could say hello, look each other over, part company and tell Leo and Faye that they have fulfilled their noble mission in life.

JENNIE: That's very funny.

GEORGE: And yet I hear no laughter.

JENNIE: Because it's not *funny* funny. It's stupid funny.

GEORGE: You think it's smart to suffer an entire evening rather than a quick five-minute "hello and goodbye"?

JENNIE: Because it's demeaning. It's like shopping. And I don't like being shopped.

GEORGE: Do you prefer window-shopping? I could stand across the street, look up and wave.

JENNIE: Am I talking to a serious person?

GEORGE: My friends tell me I have a certain charm. It's like gold, though. You have to pan for it.

Excerpt from *Chapter Two* by Neil Simon. Copyright © 1978, 1979 by the author. Reprinted by permission of Random House, Inc.

12. What had Jennie done just before George called?

(1) spoken to Leo and Faye
(2) eaten dinner
(3) taken a shower
(4) arrived home
(5) watched television

13. Based on his comments in lines 25–26, George could be classified as

(1) a hopeless romantic
(2) an impractical optimist
(3) a man who knows what he wants
(4) a power-hungry executive
(5) a fun-loving jokester

14. Why does George want to meet Jennie?

(1) He wants to satisfy his curiosity about what Jennie looks like.
(2) He thinks that he is falling in love with her.
(3) He hopes that Leo and Faye will leave them alone if they meet.
(4) He wants Leo and Faye to see for themselves the foolishness of their activities.
(5) He is amused by her clever conversation on the telephone.

Items 15 to 19 are based on the following passage.

WHY IS MAMA UNHAPPY WITH JESSIE?

MAMA: Nothing I ever did was good enough for you, and I want to know why.

JESSIE: That's not true.

MAMA: And I want to know why you've lived here this long feeling the way you do.

JESSIE: You have no earthly idea how I feel.

MAMA: Well how could I? You're real far back there, Jessie.

JESSIE: Back where?

MAMA: What's it like over there, where you are? Do people always say the right thing or get whatever they want, or what?

JESSIE: What are you talking about?

MAMA: Why do you read the newspaper? Why don't you wear that sweater I made for you? Do you remember how I used to look, or am I just any old woman now? When you have a fit do you see stars, or what? How did you fall off the horse, really? Why did Cecil leave you? Where did you put my old glasses?

JESSIE: They're in the bottom drawer of your dresser in an old Milk of Magnesia box. Cecil left me because he made me choose between him and smoking.

MAMA: Jessie, I know he wasn't that dumb.

JESSIE: I never understood why he hated it so much when it's so good. Smoking is the only thing I know that's always just what you think it's going to be. Just like it was the last time and right there when you want it and real quiet.

MAMA: Your fits made him sick, and you know it.

JESSIE: Say seizures, not fits. Seizures.

MAMA: It's the same thing. A seizure in the hospital is a fit at home.

JESSIE: They didn't bother him at all. Except he did feel responsible for it. It was his idea to go horseback riding that day. It was his idea I could do *anything* if I just made up my mind to. I fell off the horse because I didn't know how to hold on. Cecil left for pretty much the same reason.

MAMA: He had a girl, Jessie. I walked right in on them in the tool shed.

JESSIE *(after a moment)*: O.K. That's fair. *(Lights another cigarette.)* Was she very pretty?

MAMA: She was Agnes's girl, Carlene. Judge for yourself.

Excerpt from *'night Mother* by Marsha Norman. Copyright © 1983 by the author. Reprinted by permission of Hill & Wang, a division of Farrar Straus and Giroux, Inc.

15. What does the conversation between Jessie and Mama show about their relationship?

(1) They have an easygoing relationship.
(2) They do not always speak openly.
(3) They discuss their problems openly and honestly.
(4) Mama resents Jessie's success.
(5) Jessie depends too much upon Mama.

16. When Mama asks, "What's it like over there, where you are?" (lines 12-13), she is criticizing Jessie's

(1) fantasies
(2) views about marriage
(3) habit of smoking
(4) ability to provide a good home for Cecil
(5) desire to stay away from Mama's home

17. Why does Jessie smoke?

(1) She wants to irritate Mama.
(2) She wants to irritate Cecil.
(3) She is addicted to nicotine.
(4) She considers cigarettes fashionable.
(5) She considers cigarettes dependable.

18. By having Mama ask Jessie seven quick questions in a row (lines 17-25), the playwright stresses that she is feeling

(1) bored
(2) confused
(3) insecure
(4) frustrated
(5) energetic

19. Based on the conversation so far, which of the following is most likely to happen?

(1) Mama will begin to accept Jessie as she is.
(2) Jessie will have a seizure.
(3) Jessie will tell the truth about herself.
(4) Mama will continue to ask questions.
(5) Jessie will become angry about Cecil.

Items 20 to 24 are based on the following passage.

HOW DOES HIGGINS TREAT LIZA?

HIGGINS *(in despairing wrath outside)*: What the devil have I done with my slippers? *(He appears at the door.)*

LIZA *(snatching up the slippers, and hurling them at him one after the other with all her force)*: There are your slippers. And there. Take your slippers; and may you never have a day's luck with them!

HIGGINS *(astounded)*: What on earth—! *(He comes to her.)* What's the matter? Get up. *(He pulls her up.)* Anything wrong?

LIZA *(breathless)*: Nothing wrong—with you. I've won your bet for you, haven't I? That's enough for you. I don't matter, I suppose.

HIGGINS: You won my bet! You! Presumptuous insect! I won it. What did you throw those slippers at me for?

LIZA: Because I wanted to smash your face. I'd like to kill you, you selfish brute. Why didn't you leave me where you picked me out of—in the gutter? You thank God it's all over, and that now you can throw me back again there, do you? *(She crisps her fingers frantically.)*

HIGGINS *(looking at her in cool wonder)*: The creature is nervous, after all.

LIZA *(gives a suffocated scream of fury, and instinctively darts her nails at his face)*!!

HIGGINS *(catching her wrists)*: Ah! would you? Claws in, you cat. How dare you show your temper to me? Sit down and be quiet. *(He throws her roughly into the easy-chair.)*

LIZA *(crushed by superior strength and weight)*: What's to become of me? What's to become of me?

HIGGINS: How the devil do I know what's to become of you? What does it matter what becomes of you?

LIZA: You don't care. I know you don't care. You wouldn't care if I was dead. I'm nothing to you—not so much as them slippers.

HIGGINS *(thundering)*: Those slippers.

LIZA *(with bitter submission)*: Those slippers. I didn't think it made any difference now.

Excerpt from *Pygmalion* by George Bernard Shaw. Copyright ©1957. Reprinted by permission of the Society of Authors on behalf of the Bernard Shaw Estate.

20. Which of the following statements best describes the relationship between Higgins and Liza?

(1) Higgins used Liza to win a bet.
(2) Higgins and Liza are married.
(3) Higgins and Liza have known each other for years.
(4) Higgins is worried about Liza's future.
(5) Higgins is afraid of Liza.

21. Which of the following words best describes Higgins?

(1) intelligent
(2) greedy
(3) helpful
(4) stupid
(5) unfeeling

22. Liza's question "Why didn't you leave me where you picked me out of—in the gutter?" (lines 24-26), suggests that Higgins and Liza met

(1) at a roadside stand
(2) in a store
(3) by a carriage
(4) in the street
(5) at a party

23. Higgins probably would think that the idea of "equal pay for equal work" was

(1) entirely appropriate
(2) a dream for a future age
(3) an idea whose time was overdue
(4) completely idiotic
(5) acceptable under certain circumstances

24. The playwright creates sympathy for Liza rather than for Higgins by

(1) describing Liza's poor beginnings in detail
(2) having Liza pray for God's help in her difficulty
(3) having Higgins refer to her as an animal
(4) revealing Liza's emotions through stage directions rather than through dialogue
(5) revealing Higgins's emotions through dialogue alone

Items 25 to 28 are based on the following passage.

WHAT IS KEN'S PROBABLE FUTURE?

Dr. Emerson: Good... Well, Mr. Harrison, we seem to be out of the wood now...

Ken: So when are you going to discharge me?

Dr. Emerson: Difficult to say.

Ken: Really? Are you ever going to discharge me?

Dr. Emerson: Well, you'll certainly be leaving us soon, I should think.

Ken: Discharged or transferred?

Dr. Emerson: This unit is for critical patients; when we have reached a position of stability, then you can be looked after in a much more comfortable, quiet hospital.

Ken: You mean you only grow the vegetables here—the vegetable store is somewhere else.

Dr. Emerson: I don't think I understand you.

Ken: I think you do. Spell it out for me please. What chance have I of only being partly dependent on nursing?

Dr. Emerson: It's impossible to say with certainty what the prognosis of any case is.

Ken: I'm not asking for a guarantee on oath. I am simply asking for your professional opinion. Do you believe I will ever walk again?

Dr. Emerson: No.

Ken: Or recover the use of my arms?

Dr. Emerson: No.

Ken: Thank you.

Dr. Emerson: What for?

Ken: Your honesty.

Dr. Emerson: Yes, well... I should try not to brood on it if I were you. It's surprising how we can come to accept things. Dr. Scott has prescribed something which will help. *(To Dr. Scott)* You might also get Mrs. Boyle along...

Dr. Scott: Yes, of course.

Dr. Emerson: You'll be surprised how many things you will be able to do. Good morning.

Excerpt from *Whose Life Is It Anyway?* by Brian Clark. Copyright © 1978 by the author. Reprinted by permission of Judy Daish Associates, Ltd., London.

25. Where does this scene take place?

(1) in Ken's home
(2) in a hospital room
(3) in Dr. Scott's office
(4) in Dr. Emerson's office
(5) in a nursing home

26. Which of the following best describes Ken's attitude toward his disability?

(1) bitter realism
(2) uncontrollable anger
(3) cheerful optimism
(4) pretended indifference
(5) amused acceptance

27. Ken uses the word "vegetable" (lines 16-17) to refer to

(1) hospital patients
(2) the nursing staff
(3) disabled people
(4) his doctor's understanding of his problem
(5) his own condition

28. What is wrong with Ken?

(1) He has had a head injury.
(2) He has cancer.
(3) He has lost the use of his arms and legs.
(4) He has injured his legs but not his arms.
(5) He has injured his arms but not his legs.

Items 29 to 32 are based on the following passage.

WHAT DOES MORTIMER LEARN?

MORTIMER: He *was* harmless. That's why he has to go to Happy Dale. Why he has to be confined.

ABBY (*stepping to Mortimer*): Mortimer, why have you suddenly turned against Teddy—your own brother?

MORTIMER: You've got to know sometime. It might as well be now, Teddy's—killed a man!

MARTHA: Nonsense, dear.

(*Mortimer rises and points to window-seat.*)

MORTIMER: There's a body in the window-seat!

ABBY: Yes, dear, we know.

(*Mortimer "takes" as Abby and Martha busy themselves again at table.*)

MORTIMER: You *know?*

MARTHA: Of course, dear, but it has nothing to do with Teddy. (*Gets tray from side-board—arranges silver and plates on table: three places.*)

ABBY: Now, Mortimer, just forget about it—forget you ever saw the gentleman.

MORTIMER: *Forget?*

ABBY: We never dreamed you'd peek.

MORTIMER: But who is he?

ABBY: His name's Hoskins—Adam Hoskins. That's really all I know about him—except that he's Methodist.

MORTIMER: That's all you know about him? Well, what's he doing here? What happened to him?

MARTHA: He died.

MORTIMER: Aunt Martha, men don't just get into window-seats and die.

ABBY (*silly boy*): No, he died first.

MORTIMER: Well, how?

ABBY: Oh, Mortimer, don't be so inquisitive. The gentleman died because he drank some wine with poison in it.

MORTIMER: How did the poison get in the wine?

MARTHA: Well, we put it in the wine because it's less noticeable—when it's in tea it has a distinct odor.

MORTIMER: *You* put it in the wine?

ABBY: Yes. And I put Mr. Hoskins in the window-seat because Dr. Harper was coming.

MORTIMER: So you knew what you'd done! You didn't want Dr. Harper to see the body!!

ABBY: Well, not at tea—that wouldn't have been very nice. Now, Mortimer, you know the whole thing, just forget about it. I do think Martha and I have the right to our own little secrets.

Exceprt from *Arsenic and Old Lace* by Joseph Kesselring. Copyright © 1941 and renewed 1969 by Charlotte Kesserling. Reprinted by permission of Random House, Inc.

29. Which of the following questions dominates the conversation in this passage?

(1) Must Teddy go to Happy Dale?

(2) Why has Teddy killed a man?

(3) How long has Mortimer known about the murder?

(4) Why is there a body in the window-seat?

(5) How can this murder be kept a secret?

30. Who killed the man whose body is in the window-seat?

(1) Teddy

(2) Dr. Harper

(3) Martha and Abby

(4) Mortimer

(5) Adam Hoskins

31. What is "Happy Dale" (line 2)?

(1) a mental institution

(2) Teddy's best friend

(3) a holiday resort

(4) a small town

(5) a federal prison

32. By having Martha and Abby continue to set the table during the course of the conversation with Mortimer, the playwright emphasizes

(1) that they do not believe Mortimer

(2) that they do not realize what has happened

(3) that they are trying not to be terrified by what Mortimer tells them

(4) that they are not surprised to hear about the murder

(5) that they did not know the murdered man

Answers are on pages 89-91.

Poetry Items

Directions: Choose the best answer for each question.

Items 1 to 5 refer to the following poem.

WHY IS THE SPEAKER UPSET?

Absence

I visited the place where we last met.
Nothing was changed, the gardens were well-tended,
The fountains sprayed their usual jet;
There was no sign that anything had ended
And nothing to instruct me to forget.

The thoughtless birds that shook out of the trees,
Singing an ecstasy I could not share,
Played cunning in my thoughts. Sure in these
Pleasures there could not be a pain to bear
Or any discord shake the level breeze.

It was because the place was just the same
That made your absence seem a savage force,
For under all the gentleness there came
An earthquake tremor: fountain, birds and grass
Were shaken by my thinking of your name.

"Absence" by Elizabeth Jennings from *The Selected Poems of Elizabeth Jennings.*
Copyright © 1979 by Elizabeth Jennings. First published in 1979 by Carcanet New Press Ltd.
Reprinted by permission of David Higham Associates Ltd.

1. Where is the place that is spoken of in the poem?

(1) a zoo
(2) a park
(3) a museum
(4) a forest
(5) a school

2. Why does the poet call the birds "thoughtless" in line 6?

(1) They are not thinking enough about themselves.
(2) They are not aware of the beauty around them.
(3) Their singing interrupts the poet's train of thought.
(4) They do not know that an earthquake is about to happen.
(5) They are singing happily while the poet is in pain.

3. What would the speaker have preferred to find upon visiting the place described in the poem?
   (1) that the place had been changed so that she would not be reminded of her last meeting with her lover
   (2) that the birds were not singing so that she could share her pain with them
   (3) that the breeze were blowing harder so that she could not hear the birds singing
   (4) that the place seem more savage so that it would reflect her anger
   (5) that the place seem more gentle so that she would not think of her lover's name

4. What technique does the poet use to make the reader feel the strength of the speaker's emotions?
   (1) She compares the speaker's emotions to the birds in the trees that are shaken by the breeze.
   (2) She uses rhymes and rhythms in her poetry that make the reader think of earthquakes.
   (3) She uses strong language that makes the reader sympathize with the speaker's anger.
   (4) She compares the speaker's emotions to natural forces that are strong enough to affect nature.
   (5) She creates a gloomy mood by portraying nature as a reflection of the speaker's emotions.

5. Which of the following can you infer about this place from the poem?
   (1) It was the place in which the lovers parted.
   (2) It was a place in which the lovers were happy.
   (3) It was a place that made the lovers unhappy.
   (4) It was a place the speaker had kept a secret from her lover.
   (5) It was a place of unhappy memories for the speaker.

Items 6 to 10 are based on the following song lyrics.

IS SILENCE A GOOD THING OR A BAD THING?

The Sound of Silence

Hello darkness my old friend,
I've come to talk with you again,
Because a vision softly creeping,
Left its seeds while I was sleeping
And the vision that was planted in my brain
Still remains within the sound of silence.

In restless dreams I walked alone,
Narrow streets of cobblestone
'Neath the halo of a street lamp,
I turned my collar to the cold and damp
When my eyes were stabbed by the flash of a neon light
That split the night, and touched the sound of silence.

And in the naked light I saw
Ten thousand people maybe more,
People talking without speaking,
People hearing without listening,
People writing songs that voices never share
And no one dares disturb the sound of silence.

"Fools!" said I, "You do not know
Silence like a cancer grows.
Hear my words that I might teach you
Take my arms that I might reach you."
But my words like silent raindrops fell
And echoed, in the wells of silence.

And the people bowed and prayed
To the neon God they made,
And the sign flashed out its warning
In the words that it was forming.
And the sign said:
"The words of the prophets are written
on the subway walls and tenement halls"
And whispered in the sounds of silence.

"The Sound of Silence" by Paul Simon. Copyright © 1964 by Paul Simon.
Reprinted by permission of the publisher, Paul Simon Music.

6. According to the lyrics, where does the speaker experience his vision?

(1) in a dream
(2) on a walk
(3) during a conversation
(4) in the dark
(5) at a friend's

7. The details and imagery imply that the poet is mainly concerned with

(1) the horrors of war
(2) the breakdown of communication
(3) the ugliness of neon
(4) the disappearance of religion
(5) the effects of crime

8. Which of the following details would best fit in the third stanza?
   (1) "People fighting without winning"
   (2) "People sleeping without resting"
   (3) "People walking without running"
   (4) "People thinking without knowing"
   (5) "People watching without seeing"

9. The image of prophetic words on "subway walls and tenement halls" (line 31) is intended to strike a mood of
   (1) reverence
   (2) eagerness
   (3) isolation
   (4) joy
   (5) relief

10. With which of the following phrases does the poet most forceably drive home his point?
   (1) "the sound of silence"
   (2) "In restless dreams"
   (3) "in the naked light"
   (4) "I might reach you"
   (5) "flashed out its warning"

Items 11 to 14 are based on the following poem.

WHAT IS THE "LITTLE VOICE"?

your little voice
Over the wires came leaping
and i felt suddenly
dizzy
With the jostling and shouting of merry flowers
wee skipping high-heeled flames
courtesied before my eyes
or twinkling over to my side
Looked up
with impertinently exquisite faces
floating hands were laid upon me
I was whirled and tossed into delicious dancing
up
up
with the pale important
stars and Humorous
moon
dear girl
How i was crazy how i cried when i heard
over time
and tide and death
leaping
Sweetly
your voice

By e.e. cummings. Copyright © 1963, 1965 by Marion Morehouse Cummings. Reprinted by permission of Harcourt Brace Jovanovich.

11. According to the entire poem what has the speaker been doing?

(1) writing a letter to his girlfriend
(2) talking on the telephone with his girlfriend
(3) daydreaming about his girlfriend
(4) reading a letter from his girlfriend
(5) reading a story written by his girlfriend

12. Which of the following statements best summarizes the speaker's feelings?

(1) He is determined to break up with his girlfriend.
(2) He is overjoyed to be talking with his girlfriend.
(3) He no longer cares for his girlfriend.
(4) He is upset that his girlfriend is not with him.
(5) He fears that his girlfriend no longer loves him.

13. Why does the speaker use the word "up" by itself on two consecutive lines (lines 13–14)?

(1) to emphasize how small he feels
(2) to show how confused he is feeling
(3) to visually suggest how excited the speaker was
(4) to keep the lines short and easy to understand
(5) to stress how happy he used to be

14. The speaker and his girlfriend most probably

(1) are astronomers
(2) have taken too many drugs
(3) are insane
(4) live together
(5) have been apart for a while

Items 15 to 18 are based on the following poem.

WHAT KIND OF LIFE DO THE SPEAKERS LEAD?

We Real Cool

The Pool Players.
Seven at the Golden Shovel

We real cool. We
Left school. We

Lurk late. We
Strike straight. We

Sing sin. We
Think gin. We

Jazz June. We
Die soon.

"We Real Cool" by Gwendolyn Brooks. From *Blacks* by Gwendolyn Brooks. Copyright © 1959, 1991. Published by Third World Press. By permission of the author.

15. The poem is primarily about

(1) a group of college students
(2) a group of alcoholics
(3) a class of vocational students
(4) a gang of high school dropouts
(5) a band of jazz musicians

16. The poet seems to think that the pool players' life-style is

(1) elegant
(2) praiseworthy
(3) destructive
(4) artistic
(5) productive

17. Which of the following words best describes the poet's word choice?

(1) complicated
(2) informal
(3) poetic
(4) technical
(5) formal

18. What musical technique is the poet most probably imitating by using short words and lines?

(1) the slow sadness of a ballad
(2) the snappiness of jazz
(3) the softness of a love song
(4) the beat of a military march
(5) the long-drawn out notes of opera

Items 19 to 22 are based on the following poem.

WHAT DOES THE SPEAKER FEEL ABOUT THE SNOW?

Desert Places

Snow falling and night falling fast oh fast
In a field I looked into going past,
And the ground almost covered smooth in snow,
But a few weeds and stubble showing last.

The woods around it have it—it is theirs.
All animals are smothered in their lairs.
I am too absent-spirited to count;
The loneliness includes me unawares.

And lonely as it is that loneliness
Will be more lonely ere it will be less—
A blanker whiteness of benighted snow
With no expression, nothing to express.

They cannot scare me with their empty spaces
Between stars—on stars where no human race is.
I have it in me so much nearer home
To scare myself with my own desert places.

From *The Poetry of Robert Frost* edited by Edward Connery Lathem.
Copyright © 1936 by Robert Frost. Copyright © 1964 by Lesley Frost Ballantine.
Copyright © 1969 by Holt, Rinehart and Winston. Reprinted by permission of Henry Holt and Company, Inc.

19. The word "benighted" (line 11) means

(1) getting a knighthood
(2) covered by the darkness of night
(3) turning white with fear
(4) smothered to death
(5) melted

20. To what does the "it" in line 5 refer?

(1) the snow
(2) the ground
(3) the weeds
(4) the field
(5) the woods

21. The poem suggests that the speaker is feeling

(1) tired
(2) satisfied
(3) angry
(4) cheerful
(5) lonely

22. The choice of the expression "desert places" is meant to impress the reader with

(1) the horrors of life that the speaker once led
(2) the beauty of landscape through which the speaker is traveling
(3) the empty space that exists between the stars
(4) the emptiness that the speaker feels
(5) the bitterness of cold and snow that accompany winter

Items 23 to 26 are based on the following poem.

DOES THE PRISONER HAVE A FUTURE?

Bread

He had been imprisoned
for so many years,
time was a chain around his neck
knotted up in the windings of his life.

A piece of bread
and a can of broth
are left at the door by the guard,
he grabs them with dirty hands.

When the wretched man
is about to swallow,
the tear-soaked bread drops,
rubbing against the bruise in his heart

He remembers why
he was imprisoned:
he stole a box of crackers
because his sick child was groaning with hunger

Trying to get away
from the fist of the law
he killed his pursuer—
and never saw his little girl again!

Now life wears away
wearily, though now every day
he is given the bread that might have saved
his child, who died of hunger.

"Bread" by Amado V. Hernandez. Translated by E. San Juan, Jr.
Copyright © 1966 by International Publishers. Reprinted by permission.

23. Why was the man sent to prison?

(1) He was caught stealing and then killed an officer.

(2) He started a riot.

(3) He mistreated his children.

(4) He impersonated an officer of the law.

(5) He protested unjust laws.

24. What is "the bruise in his heart" (line 12)?

(1) the illness that he has contracted in prison

(2) the beatings he has received from the prison guards

(3) his sadness about his daughter

(4) his memories of his happiness before going to prison

(5) his misery in thinking about the future

25. The poet sets up a striking contrast by revealing that

(1) the government that put the man in prison was overthrown only a few days later

(2) several of the man's fellow prisoners had been jailed for the same crimes

(3) the prisoner has become so numbed by beatings that the guards can no longer hurt him

(4) the prisoner's daughter is now living with the family of the officer who had chased him

(5) the prisoner has his food supplied whereas his daughter has starved to death

26. Which of the following words best describes the feeling the poet wants the reader to experience in this poem?

(1) bright hope

(2) bitter helplessness

(3) cautious optimism

(4) deep reverence

(5) mild frustration

Items 27 to 30 are based on the following poem.

WHAT PROBLEMS DOES THE SPEAKER FACE?

Cotton Candy On A Rainy Day

Don't look now
I'm fading away
Into the gray of my mornings
Or the blues of every night

Is it that my nails
  keep breaking
Or maybe the corn
  on my second little piggy
Things keep popping out
  on my face
      or
  of my life

It seems no matter how
I try I become more difficult
  to hold
I am not an easy woman
  to want

They have asked
  the psychiatrists   psychologists   politicians and
  social workers
What this decade will be
  known for
There is no doubt   it is
  loneliness

From *"Cotton Candy On A Rainy Day"* by Nikki Giovanni. Copyright © 1978 by the author. Reprinted by permission of William Morrow & Company, Inc. Publishers.

27. What does the speaker show by beginning with the words "Don't look now" (line 1)?

(1) She wants to warn the reader against what is happening to her.
(2) She desperately wants someone to help her.
(3) She is ashamed of what is happening to her.
(4) She wants the world's attention when she gets over her problem.
(5) She is surprised by the problem she is facing.

28. Which colors does the speaker use to express her feelings?

(1) gray and red
(2) black and white
(3) black and blue
(4) pink and blue
(5) blue and gray

29. The unusual comparison in "Things keep popping out/on my face/or/of my life" (lines 9–12) is intended to let the reader sense

(1) the speaker's wish to conquer her problem
(2) the speaker's feeling of losing control
(3) the social workers' view of the future for the poor
(4) the psychologists' view of the mentally ill
(5) the view that other people have of the speaker

30. Which of the following is most probably the poet's reason for the length of the line "the psychiatrists psychologists politicians and" (line 19)?

(1) to create a break in the rhyme scheme
(2) to highlight the failure of so-called experts
(3) to explain who the speaker talked to
(4) to predict what the speaker will become
(5) to show how the speaker is solving her problem

Answers are on pages 91–93.

Commentary Items

Directions: Choose the one best answer for each question.

Items 1 to 5 are based on the following passage.

WHAT'S HAPPENING ON THE NASHVILLE NETWORK?

Once and for all, country music has shed its *Hee Haw* past. If you want proof—in case last season's super ratings for a Garth Brooks concert special are not enough—turn on The Nashville Network and you'll see no corn pone, no hay. You'll see people having a great time.

I just started getting TNN on my cable, after years without it, and it has become my latest favorite channel. TNN is filled with videos in the A.M. and P.M. and lots of talk shows the rest of the time (the best: *Crook and Chase*, country's Regis and Kathie Lee with flashier wardrobes). I watch TNN's *Remodeling & Decorating Today* (it beats the tar out of *This Old House*) and both its kicky cooking shows (*Country Kitchen* stars Florence Henderson, who's never far from her trusty bottle of Wesson Oil). I love *American Music Shop*, country's *Unplugged*. But right now, my favorite show on my favorite channel is *Club Dance*—because, more than anything else on TV, it's a show about having fun.

Every afternoon, a few hundred folks fill a Knoxville studio to dance the two-step, the Tush Push (if you don't know how to do it, commercials will offer you lessons on videotape), and the latest line-dance craze, the Achy Breaky.

Unlike other dance shows—from *American Bandstand* to *Soul Train* to the late *Club MTV*—this one doesn't select who'll twirl on camera based on the hipness of their clothes; here, you'll see plenty of big bellies and big plaids, lots of frills and fringe. Some of these people can dance like Flying country Wallendas—but some can't. One day, a little old lady complained that nobody had asked her to dance, so she was paired with a *Club* regular for a spin; another day, a tubby and brave kid got his first dancing lesson right there on the show.

So they're not all hunky and young; *Club Dance* proves that country music has long since rid itself of a generation gap (which is only now happening to rock music). The *Club* also proves that country music is hospitable. Anybody can come down and join in. You don't have to be Southern (*Club*sters are as likely from Montreal or even New Jersey). And you don't have to be cool. When *Club* hostess and country dream Shelley Mangrum wanders the floor between numbers, chatting with folks, it reminds me of the good old days when a TV camera still made people nervous and shy. These are real people. They're not here for publicity. They're here for fun.

So when you get depressed watching the Presidential campaign this summer—who wouldn't?—do what I do for relief: turn to TNN and *Club Dance* for music you can dance and smile to.

From "Club Dance" by Jeff Jarvis, reprinted with permission from *TV Guide*® Magazine. Copyright © 1992 News America Publications, Inc.

1. What type of music is played on *Club Dance*?

(1) soul
(2) country
(3) classical
(4) oldies but goodies
(5) hard rock

2. Which of the following best describes the dancers on the show?
   (1) professional
   (2) skilled
   (3) beginners
   (4) hip
   (5) varied

3. The author seems to feel that, as a television series, Club Dance
   (1) has no possibility of success
   (2) has a very limited appeal
   (3) is high-class
   (4) is enjoyable
   (5) makes people nervous

4. The author mentions the two-step, Tush Push and Achy Breaky (paragraph three) in order to
   (1) give an example of the fun people have on the show
   (2) explain why he likes TNN programs
   (3) compare *Remodeling & Decorating Today* with *This Old House*
   (4) describe *American Music Shop*
   (5) demonstrate the lack of a generation gap

5. Which of the following would be the best title for this review?
   (1) Moving Forward and Loving It
   (2) The Death of Country Music
   (3) Dances for the Young
   (4) Country Stands Still
   (5) The Return of American Bandstand

Items 6 to 10 are based on the following passage.

WHAT DOES RING LARDNER'S FICTION REVEAL ABOUT THE MAN?

Vanity, greed, and cruel humor are the themes of Lardner's stories. The lack of self-knowledge is made up for by a dizzy readiness with cheap alibis. No group or class seems better than another; there is a democracy of cheapness and shallowness. Lies are at the core of nearly every character he produces for us. The only fear is being caught out, exposed to the truth. Love cannot exist because the moment it runs into trouble the people lie about their former feelings. Because of the habit of lying, it is a world without common sense. The tortured characters are not always victims. They may be ruined and made fun of, but they have the last word. They bite the leg that kicks them.

"Haircut" is one of the cruelest pieces of American fiction. Even Lardner seems to have felt some need for relief from the relentless evil of the smalltown joker and so he has him killed in the end. This cruel story is just about the only one that has the contrast of decent people preyed upon by a maniac. "Champion" is brutal and "The Golden Honeymoon" is a masterpiece of grim realism. Alfred Kazin speaks of the "harsh, glazed coldness" of Lardner's work. He wrapped his dreadful events in a comic language, as you would put an insecticide in a bright can.

Lardner's personality is very difficult to take hold of. In spite of poor health that came, so far as I can discover, from his devastating drinking, he had the continuing productivity of the professional journalist. He went to work every morning. Why he drank, why his views were so bitter are a mystery. He came from a charming, talented family and married a woman he loved. He was kind, reserved, hard-working; his fictional world is loud, cruel, filled with desperate marriages, hideous old age, suburban wretchedness, fraud, drunkenness. Even the sports world is degraded and athletes are likely to be sadists, crooks, or dumbbells. The vision is thoroughly desperate. All the literature of the thirties and forties does not contain such pure subversion, snatched on the run from the common man and his old jokes.

"Lives and Social Scenery" from *Bartleby in Manhattan and Other Essays* by Elizabeth Hardwick. Copyright © 1983 by Elizabeth Hardwick. Reprinted with permission of Random House, Inc.

6. The passage describes the characters who appear in Lardner's fiction as generally
   (1) charming
   (2) incomprehensible
   (3) compassionate
   (4) horrible
   (5) thoughtful

7. According to lines 28–32, Alfred Kazin viewed Lardner as
   (1) a pessimistic writer
   (2) a cheerful writer
   (3) a gifted writer
   (4) an amusing writer
   (5) a realistic writer

8. In which of the following ways does the author sum up Ring Lardner as a person?
   (1) a useless drunk
   (2) a cruel and greedy man
   (3) a victim
   (4) an evil joker
   (5) a mystery

9. The author's statement "He wrapped his dreadful events in a comic language, as you would put insecticide in a bright can" (lines 30-32) is meant to stress which aspect of Lardner's work?
   (1) its deadly bitterness
   (2) its local color
   (3) its hidden optimism
   (4) its bright imagery
   (5) its skillful conciseness

10. Which of the following TV shows would the reviewer be least likely to enjoy?
   (1) a situation comedy
   (2) a drama based on a true story
   (3) a variety show
   (4) a program based on the confessions of a serial killer
   (5) an early morning news show

Items 11 to 15 are based on the following passage.

ARE NORMAN ROCKWELL'S PAINTINGS GREAT ART?

We can say, first, last, and always, that Norman Rockwell has been true to his beginnings, to his trust in his own and American sentiment. He is a genre painter; he uses graphic means to tell a story. His technique may be described as the most perfect where it dissolves, imperceptibly, into anecdote. This anecdotal picture that tells a simple story is the father of the story that gives us the simple picture, the *same* picture, as a rule—an unadorned, unpretentious, photographically convincing portrayal of *real* life.

In a period of forty years Rockwell has supplied the *Post* with more than three hundred of its covers. He has taught a generation of Americans to see. They look about them and see, almost everywhere they look, what Norman Rockwell sees—the tomboy with black eye in the doctor's waiting room; the father discussing the Facts of Life with his teen-age son; the youth in the dining car on his first solo flight from home; and the family in the car, headed for an outing, followed by the same family on the tired ride home.

The convincing *realism* of the details, photographic in its accuracy, is all subtly processed through a filter of sentiment. It is this sentiment that heightens the reality, making it, for some, an object of affection, for others—a small minority—an object of ridicule. It all depends on that intangible thing the point of view.

Countless young men and women at the beginning of careers in art, have tried, and usually failed, to explain *their* point of view to a puzzled mother, a skeptical father. What can be wrong—Father would like to know—with Norman Rockwell, who is so obviously *good*? The answer is his very *goodness*, of course, but this usually ends the argument. Discussion leads nowhere. The two points of view go their different ways.

From "Abuse of the Past: Norman Rockwell" by Wright Morris. Copyright by the author. Reprinted by permission of the author and Harcourt Brace Jovanovich.

11. According to the author, Norman Rockwell is often remembered as

(1) an abstract painter
(2) a sentimental painter
(3) a subtle painter
(4) a misunderstood painter
(5) an unsuccessful painter

12. The author feels that Rockwell did his best work when

(1) his painting told a story
(2) his painting was open to several interpretations
(3) he worked for *The Saturday Evening Post*
(4) he was a young man
(5) he had just gone through a difficult problem

13. You can conclude that Rockwell was popular with a generation of Americans because his paintings

(1) challenged the imagination
(2) were praised by other artists
(3) reflected their own experience of life
(4) were published in the *Post*
(5) were based on photographs

14. The author illustrates the realism in Rockwell's work by

(1) contrasting Rockwell with other painters
(2) discussing Rockwell's use of color and shadow
(3) discussing Rockwell's unusual amount of decoration in his work
(4) quoting Rockwell's own view of the subject
(5) listing the subjects of several of Rockwell's paintings

15. By imagining a conversation between young art students and their parents (lines 40-46), the author impresses the reader with the fact that

(1) most people agree about Rockwell's art
(2) Rockwell's art is a good subject for stimulating conversation
(3) art students know much more about art than their parents do
(4) people disagree strongly about the value of Rockwell's art
(5) Rockwell's art usually is criticized unfairly

Items 16 to 20 are based on the following passage.

HOW BAD ARE AMERICAN MOVIES?

The death of American movies has been announced many times before. It was announced in the early sound period, when the camera stopped moving; in the forties, when the clean family films stifled those moviegoers accustomed to the looser, jazzier pictures of the thirties; in the late forties, when television came in and everyone got scared; in the fifties, when the wide screen (a response to television) momentarily destroyed the art of composition; and in the late sixties, when the big studios produced too many expensive flops. It was announced, in a very convincing way, by Pauline Kael, in a *New Yorker* column called "Why Are Movies So Bad? or, The Numbers," a furious little polemic that she composed six years ago in 1981, after a year spent in Hollywood. The earlier announcements of death were, as Mark Twain put it, greatly exaggerated. But Kael, who described the pathology of Hollywood in the era of conglomerate control, now appears to have been right in assuming that certain trends were irreversible. And since she wrote her piece, everything has grown much worse. There are many new reasons to be gloomy about the studios.

Even if we're aware of the dangers of prophecy, it's been hard not to feel, in recent years, that something portentous and truly awful has been happening. Critics are not the only ones who say so. Many adult moviegoers—and perhaps some of the kids, too—look at what's playing and feel abandoned and betrayed. They continue going, of course, because they have to go to *something*, but they aren't necessarily happy. American movies, the liveliest in the world a decade ago, have become an object of contempt. Judging from what I hear in theaters, in supermarkets, at the beach, around town, almost everyone, at some level, senses that our movies have been trivialized, infantilized, massified, and marketed to death. "Movies don't have the place in the national heart that they did twenty, ten, maybe even five years ago," Tom Shales wrote in the July *Esquire*. No, and not in the national soul either. And we're not just talking of a bad season or year, but of every season and every year. And not just of a few ailing companies, but of an industry that has *rendered itself incapable of bringing out more than five or six interesting movies a year*. At the moment, the only thing the system does well is market.

From "Can The Movies Be Saved?" by David Denby. Copyright © 1986 K-III Magazine Corporation. Reprinted by permission.

16. According to the author, a recent announcement of the death of American movies occurred

(1) in the late 1960s
(2) just after World War II
(3) in 1981
(4) in the early sound period
(5) during the Great Depression

17. The information in the passage suggests that the author

(1) is pessimistic about the future of American movies
(2) does not believe the negative criticisms of American movies
(3) feels that American movies will improve in the near future
(4) hopes that the American public will protest until movies improve
(5) believes that American movies have always been bad

18. Based on the article, you can tell that the author

(1) wants to be an actor
(2) objects to all movie critics
(3) has not seen many movies
(4) doesn't know much about movie history
(5) knows a lot about the history of movies

19. The author would probably say that movie studios have become most like

(1) playwrights
(2) religious leaders
(3) advertising companies
(4) book publishers
(5) television show producers

20. Quoting Tom Shales's comment on movies (lines 48–51) allows the author to

(1) emphasize his disagreement with Shales
(2) support his argument
(3) illustrate the different opinions people have about current movies
(4) show how mistaken Shales has been in the past
(5) reveal how movies have changed since Shales's statement

Items 21 to 25 are based on the following passage.

ARE PEOPLE HAPPY WITH THE QUALITY OF TELEVISION?

Our mass media, the movies as well as radio and television, offer a greater variety of entertainments, but they are for the most part aimed at the same intellectual level and call for the same emotional responses, the level and the responses being relatively low. The challenge to the mind comes infrequently, and we are being conditioned to make frequent emotional responses of low intensity—the quick nervous reaction to melodrama and the quick laugh at everything else. If material cannot be adapted to give the thrill or the laugh, it is thrown out. A spectacular instance of this occurred recently in the Ford anniversary show, where the entire story of life in the United States in the past half century was reduced to vaudeville, the violent strikes of the 1920's being presented as part of a jocular newsreel, the Depression in a ballet, and the revolution of the New Deal, being intractable, omitted entirely. It was a very successful program, and its success is part of the conditioning process which I call creative, by which the audience is persuaded that it is getting all it can ever want.

Statistical evidence exists that actually the audience—the public, to be more accurate—wants more. I place few bets on the automatic answer given to researchers, "Yes, we would like more serious programs on the air," because, for one thing, some of the responders call quiz shows educational and because this "want" is a pious aspiration as diffused and uncertain as what the broadcasters say they get from the public. Yet it is noteworthy that *all* the researchers point in the same direction: people at every level of education, in significant numbers, do imply some dissatisfaction with the programs they are getting, and among these there are ten million people, not habitual book readers, not college graduates, who consistently ask for programs of a higher intellectual content.

"Radio, TV, and The Common Man" from *Is The Common Man Too Common? An Informal Survey of Our Cultural Resources and What We Are Doing About Them,* by Joseph Wood Krutch and others. Copyright © 1954, by Univ. of Oklahoma Press, and reprinted by permission.

21. What is the main idea of the passage?

(1) that the quality of TV shows has been steadily improving
(2) that most people are not satisfied with the quality of TV shows
(3) that only educated people would like to see better TV shows
(4) that television shows will always be low in quality
(5) that most people are satisfied with the quality of TV shows

22. You can infer from the context in which it is used that the word "intractable" (paragraph one) probably means

(1) difficult to manage
(2) complex
(3) difficult to understand
(4) controversial
(5) political in nature

23. According to the article, the reason for the success of the Ford anniversary show is most similar to the reason for the success of

(1) new model sportscars
(2) fast-food restaurants
(3) the nation-wide literacy program
(4) foreign automobiles
(5) the computer industry

24. By saying that the Ford anniversary show reduced 50 years of American history to "vaudeville," the author is emphasizing that the show

(1) explained American history clearly
(2) falsified American history
(3) made American history more entertaining
(4) ignored American history
(5) trivialized American history

25. The author suggests that the mass media do not provide

(1) cheap thrills
(2) entertainment
(3) historical programs
(4) quick laughs
(5) serious programs

Items 26 to 30 are based on the following passage.

WHAT IS ADVENTUROUS ABOUT THIS McDONALD'S BUILDING?

No one associates architectural adventure with McDonald's, under whose golden arches more than 50 billion hamburgers have been consumed since its founding 36 years ago. Over the years, the chain has commissioned nothing but carbon-copy buildings; nearly all of its 8,000 fast-food restaurants in 33 countries sport the same rustic mansard roof, walls of warm red brick and windows that are cosily colonial. So what happens when the hamburger giant puts itself in the hands of the most audacious architects alive? The provocative—and tremendously popular—answer is now on view in a Berwyn, Ill., shopping center near Chicago. Challenged by mall owner David Bermant to come up with a more daring design, McDonald's reluctantly agreed to commission three radical New York-based designers named Alison Sky, Michelle Stone and James Wines. Collectively known as SITE, their firm strikes fear in the heart of the gray-flannel architecture profession. It is notorious for radical reversals, for buildings whose facades seem to be crumbling apart or tilting on their sides or that are "invaded" by hungry trees, plants and vines.

Radical reversal is precisely what SITE has done to McDonald's standard design. While all the familiar parts are still there, they are dramatically altered. From afar, the new emporium seems poised for flight. The roof floats weightlessly above the rest of the building. Parts of the facade are raised above the ground on unobtrusive steel piers; the resulting gaps are paneled with glass, exposing the feet and legs of customers inside to passers-by. The customers can enjoy a view of the sky through the glass clerestory just below the building's roof. Dubbed "The Floating McDonald's," the razzle-dazzle structure is attracting gapers and tourists. For the first time, McDonald's is a magnet for devotees of architecture as well as of hamburgers.

From "McDonald's With A Difference" by Douglas Davis. Copyright © 1984 by *Newsweek*. Reprinted by permission.

26. The topic of this passage is a discussion of

(1) the popularity of McDonald's hamburgers
(2) SITE, an unusual architectural company
(3) the effect of McDonald's buildings on consumers
(4) a new and unusual McDonald's building
(5) the history of radical architecture

27. In its context, the term "gray-flannel" (line 24) means

(1) wealthy
(2) conservative
(3) incompetent
(4) daring
(5) radical

28. Which of the following words best describes the look of the new McDonald's?

(1) crumbling
(2) airy
(3) quaint
(4) tilting
(5) impersonal

29. According to the author, the idea of having a new design for the building began with

(1) David Bermant
(2) Alison Sky
(3) Michelle Stone and James Wine
(4) SITE
(5) McDonald's

30. If the author were to commission a design for a new home, he probably would want it

(1) to make good use of the available greenery
(2) to include a skylight
(3) to be functional but visually interesting
(4) to look very futuristic
(5) to be as different as possible from the other homes in the neighborhood

Items 31 to 35 are based on the following passage.

WHAT IS HAPPENING IN THIS MAN'S WORLD?

In the heart of the world where Naguib Mahfouz grew up there is a neighborhood of hidden palaces called Gemaliya. To get there from Cairo's bazaar you must pass the Huasayn Mosque, where the beggars hold out leprous hands. From inside come the chanting voices of men in prayer. Follow the snaking alleys and twisted streets, where flies swarm among the crumbling villas, and women in black robes look out from the skewed sills of ancient windows as you pass.

There is no Baedeker's guide to this quarter. There are only the novels of Mahfouz to show you the way. The alleys, the houses, the palaces and mosques and the people who live among them are evoked as vividly in his work as the streets of London were conjured up by Dickens. Mahfouz, now 78, won the Nobel Prize in Literature in 1988 for his stories about this world, the first Arab ever to be given the honor. Yet his greatest books—"The Cairo Trilogy," which span three generations of one Gemaliya family—have never been available in English. Now at last the first volume, **Palace Walk** (498 pages. Doubleday. $22.95), has come out in the United States, in a good translation by William M. Hutchins and Olive E. Kenny.

"Palace Walk," first published in 1956, is the best of Mahfouz's work. He drew heavily on autobiography (like the character Kamal, he was the youngest son in a large merchant clan). He writes about family, and to understand the Egyptian family is to understand, more clearly than any political treatise can explain, the soul of the country.

The family in "Palace Walk" is tested by its own internal tensions and by the political tumult of Egypt at the end of World War I. The sexual passions of one son and the political passions of another threaten to tear the home apart. But the mother holds everything together. At first she seems a pitiful figure—married at 14 and forbidden forever to venture outside her home. She "knew far more about the world of the jinn than that of mankind and remained convinced that she was not alone in the big house." But her strength lies in her intimacy with the family's secrets. "She had no regrets about reconciling herself to a type of security based on surrender," writes Mahfouz. Her one effort at escape is an act of piety that ends in disaster.

Mahfouz's newfound recognition in the West comes after a life filled with fame and controversy in the Arab world. He helped invent the modern novel in Arabic: His books gained him critical success among his peers, and the movies made from them gained him an enormous audience. But the frank realism of his characters, especially the women, gained him the hatred of religious zealots.

The Nobel laureate seems unconcerned, living as he has for decades in the same flat by the Nile. Diabetic, his eyes weak and his hearing waning, he follows a daily routine that takes him from his favorite coffee house to his office at one of the semiofficial newspapers, then occasionally for chats with friends in tea gardens near the river. Sometimes, pressed for interviews by journalists, hounded by academics looking for fleeting insights into his work, Mahfouz complains he has become "a prisoner of the prize." But he does not worry much about the fundamentalists, and he refuses bodyguards. "At my age, a threat of death is not really that frightening," he says. "I might receive a threat on Sunday and die on Monday of natural causes."

From Christopher Dickey, "A Baedeker to Egypt's Soul," in *Newsweek,* February 26, 1990, copyright © 1990 Newsweek, Inc. Reprinted by permission.

31. Where is the novel, *Palace Walk,* set?
- **(1)** London, England
- **(2)** Cairo, Egypt
- **(3)** tea gardens near the Nile River
- **(4)** Egyptian newspaper offices
- **(5)** the mind of an Egyptian mother

32. Which of the following is NOT true of Naguib Mahfouz?
- **(1)** He won a Nobel Prize.
- **(2)** His novels were not written in English.
- **(3)** He has influenced the modern Arabic novel.
- **(4)** He is admired by religious zealots.
- **(5)** He is not afraid of threats.

33. Mahfouz sometimes is bothered by journalists and scholars because
- **(1)** religious fundamentalists are making threats against his life
- **(2)** he has made a number of movies
- **(3)** he works at a semiofficial newspaper
- **(4)** he has become famous in both the Arab world and the West
- **(5)** he is a prisoner

34. The first and last paragraph of this article give a sense of
- **(1)** the importance of autobiographies
- **(2)** where Mahfouz came from and what he does now
- **(3)** why Mahfouz became a writer
- **(4)** the contents of Mahfouz's trilogy
- **(5)** the source of conflict in the Mid-East

35. With which of the following would Mahfouz most probably agree?
- **(1)** Politics can destroy a family.
- **(2)** The family is the basic unit of society.
- **(3)** The family unit is no longer useful.
- **(4)** Women have no importance in the Arab world.
- **(5)** Religion plays no part in the Arab world.

Items 36 to 40 are based on the following passage.

WHAT HAD TIRED BLOOD?

"Fangs a lot," loyal fans said when NBC exhumed *Dark Shadows* with a four-hour TV-movie in January. The Dan Curtis resuscitation of his original Gothic soap opera (which ran from 1966 to 1971 on ABC) had to be the major cultural event of the second season: I hear it got virtually 93 percent of the sets in use in vampires' homes.

A couch-potato vampire myself, I gave the revival four stakes. The remake, I thought, was well done if you like vampire stories. It was a slice of surreal life, technically superior to the original. The cast actually memorized their lines.

Every cliché of every vampire story filmed was here—the casket, the chains, the mist on the moor, the thunder cracking. You could fill in every word of dialogue and howl with laughter.

But the new, improved *Dark Shadows* didn't have the addictive quality of the original. I saw it once that Sunday night in January and had no real inclination to watch it anymore. One bite and you've seen them all.

Still, I watched the tapes out of morbid curiosity. The regular weekly episodes of Friday nights at 9 (ET) have been disappointing. Maybe it's because of Ben Cross, who plays Barnabas Collins in a potentially dangerous career move. Love his orthodontia and those sexy red eyes. But he is not campy fun, like Jonathan Frid.

One disconcerting twist is seeing Barnabas walking around in the daylight. It's amazing what a dab of No. 15 sunscreen can do.

And how about the Collinsport Police Department using crosses and a wooden stake to drive into the heart of Barnabas's undead victim Daphne (Rebecca Staab) (R.I.P.)? The police in Maine are so open to the latest scientific technology.

The series did pick up with the arrival of Angelique (Lysette Anthony) and the return to 1790 in the seventh episode (Feb. 8). Almost everybody took on a new role, adding new meaning to the show's most immortal line so far, uttered by Willie (Jim Fyfe), Barnabas's Jeeves: "Jeez, Barnabas, what's going on?"

It's goofy. But not goofy enough. Neither is it strange and weird like early *Twin Peaks*. The police, for example, in the first five killings never once check the fingertips to see if there are any letter B's under the nails of the victims. What kind of cops are those?

Maybe it's because I, unlike Barnabas, have aged. I'm no longer 13, when I last really dug the show. I'm just not going batty over the new *Dark Shadows*. Blame it all on tired blood.

From *"Shadows* Doesn't Have Enough Bite," in *TV Guide,* March 2, 1991. Reprinted with permission from TV Guide® Magazine. Copyright © 1991 by News America Publications, Inc.

36. What main point did the reviewer want to make in this article?

(1) TV audiences aren't interested in vampire shows.

(2) He preferred the series to the movie remake.

(3) He enjoyed the changes in the new series.

(4) He was disappointed in the new series.

(5) Vampire movies are best when the actors know their lines.

37. Based on the references to the early *Dark Shadows* series, you can tell that the reviewer

(1) had never seen it

(2) was a fan of the original *Dark Shadows*

(3) would like anything to do with vampires

(4) thought the original soap opera was awful

(5) had a bit part in the soap opera

38. What kinds of characters would this reviewer probably have wanted to see in the remake of *Dark Shadows*?

(1) spooky but goofy
(2) totally predictable
(3) grim and depressing
(4) more up-to-date
(5) unbelievable

39. The reviewer uses words such as "exhumed" (line 2), "resuscitation" (line 4), and "four stakes" (line 11) to describe the show in order to

(1) humorously refer to the content of the program
(2) imply that he is a vampire too
(3) scare the reader
(4) improve the readers' knowledge about vampires
(5) appeal to doctors

40. Which of the following was the reviewer most likely to have said when this show was finally cancelled?

(1) "What a shame!"
(2) "Bring it back!"
(3) "Good riddance to bad rubbish!"
(4) "Fangs for trying, but I'm not surprised."
(5) "Who cares?"

Answers are on pages 93–96.

Half-length Practice Test

Directions: Choose the one best answer for each question.

Items 1 to 4 are based on the following passage.

WHAT DISCOVERY HAS THE WOMAN MADE?

The first day I did not think it was funny. I didn't think it was funny the third day either, but I managed to make a little joke about it. "The most unfair thing about this whole business," I said, "is that I can't even date." Well, you had to be there, as they say, because when I put it down on paper it doesn't sound funny. But what made it funny (trust me) is the word "date," which when you say it out loud at the end of a sentence has a wonderful teenage quality, and since I am not a teenager (okay, I'm thirty-eight), and since the reason I was hardly in a position to date on first learning that my second husband had taken a lover was that I was seven months pregnant, I got a laugh on it, though for all I know my group was only laughing because they were trying to cheer me up. I was in New York, staying in my father's apartment, I was crying most of the time, and every time I stopped crying I had to look at my father's incredibly depressing walnut furniture and slate-gray lamps, which made me start crying again.

I had gotten on the shuttle to New York a few hours after discovering the affair, which I learned about from a really disgusting inscription to my husband in a book of children's songs she had given him. *Children's* songs. "Now you can sing these songs to Sam" was part of the disgusting inscription, and I can't begin to tell you how it sent me up the wall, the idea of my two-year-old child, my baby, involved in some dopey inscriptive way in this affair between my husband, a fairly short person, and Thelma Rice, a fairly tall person with a neck as long as an arm and a nose as long as a thumb and you should see her legs, never mind her feet, which are sort of splayed.

From *Heartburn* by Nora Ephron. Copyright © 1983 by the author. Reprinted by permission of Random House, Inc.

1. Why does the speaker think she can't date?

(1) She is married.
(2) She is afraid of men.
(3) She is seven months pregnant.
(4) Her friends would laugh at her.
(5) Her father has forbidden it.

2. Which of the following words best describes the narrator's state of mind?

(1) happy
(2) upset
(3) relieved
(4) indifferent
(5) hopeful

3. If the narrator's boss told her she was fired, how would she probably respond?

(1) cautiously
(2) passively
(3) emotionally
(4) thoughtfully
(5) quietly

4. Which of the following words best describes the author's attitude in this passage?

(1) humorous
(2) sad
(3) unemotional
(4) cautious
(5) serious

Items 5 to 8 are based on the following passage.

WHAT DOES MRS. FLOWERS WANT THE NARRATOR TO LEARN?

Mrs. Bertha Flowers was the aristocrat of Black Stamps. She had the grace of control to appear warm in the coldest weather, and on the Arkansas summer days it seemed she had a private breeze which swirled around, cooling her. She was thin without the taut look of wiry people, and her printed voile dresses and flowered hats were as right for her as denim overalls for a farmer. She was our side's answer to the richest white woman in town.

The sweet scent of vanilla had met us as she opened the door.

"I made tea cookies this morning. You see, I had planned to invite you for cookies and lemonade so we could have this little chat. The lemonade is in the icebox."

It followed that Mrs. Flowers would have ice on an ordinary day, when most families in our town bought ice late on Saturdays only a few times during the summer to be used in the wooden ice-cream freezers.

As I ate she began the first of what we later called "my lessons in living." She said that I must always be intolerant of ignorance but understanding of illiteracy. That some people, unable to go to school, were more educated and even more intelligent than college professors. She encouraged me to listen carefully to what country people called mother wit. That in those homely sayings was couched the collective wisdom of generations.

When I finished the cookies she brushed off the table and brought a thick, small book from the bookcase. I had read *A Tale of Two Cities* and found it up to my standards as a romantic novel. She opened the first page and I heard poetry for the first time in my life.

"It was the best of times and the worst of times..." Her voice slid in and curved down through and over the words. She was nearly singing. I wanted to look at the pages. Were they the same that I had read? Or were there notes, music, lined on the pages, as in a hymn book? Her sounds began cascading gently. I knew from listening to a thousand preachers that she was nearing the end of her reading, and I hadn't really heard, heard to understand, a single word.

"How do you like that?"

It occurred to me that she expected a response. The sweet vanilla flavor was still on my tongue and her reading was a wonder in my ears. I had to speak.

I said, "Yes, ma'am." It was the least I could do, but it was the most also.

Excerpt from *I Know Why The Caged Bird Sings* by Maya Angelou. Copyright © 1969 by the author. Reprinted by permission of Random House, Inc.

5. From the description of Mrs. Flowers, it can be inferred that

(1) she is more refined than her neighbors
(2) she owns the town bakery
(3) she is an aged widow
(4) the townspeople are suspicious of her
(5) the narrator does not know who she really is

6. What effect does hearing Mrs. Flowers read *A Tale of Two Cities* have on the narrator?

(1) She decides to become a writer.
(2) She decides the novel is up to her romantic standards.
(3) She starts to understand the power of writing.
(4) She realizes how wonderful the human voice is.
(5) She becomes a fan of music.

7. Which of the following best describes the speaker's attitude toward Mrs. Flowers?

(1) She thinks that Mrs. Flowers is too arrogant.

(2) She is afraid of Mrs. Flowers.

(3) She admires Mrs. Flowers.

(4) She doesn't understand Mrs. Flowers' ideas.

(5) Mrs. Flowers makes her feel unimportant.

8. How does the author emphasize the importance of Mrs. Flowers?

(1) by telling what the country people say about her

(2) by describing the food she serves

(3) by saying she was the black community's answer to a rich white woman

(4) by having the narrator sit beneath her portrait

(5) by speaking of her from a child's point of view

Items 9 to 12 are based on the following passage.

WHAT DOES FRANKIE DISCOVER ABOUT HERSELF?

JOHN HENRY: What you thinking about?

FRANKIE: About the wedding. About my brother and the bride. Everything's been so sudden today. I never believed before about the fact that the earth turns at the rate of about a thousand miles a day. I didn't understand why it was that if you jumped up in the air you wouldn't land in Selma or Fairview or somewhere else instead of the same back yard. But now it seems to me I feel the world going around very fast. (FRANKIE *begins turning around in circles with arms outstretched.* JOHN HENRY *copies her. They both turn.*) I feel it turning and it makes me dizzy.

JOHN HENRY: I'll stay and spend the night with you.

FRANKIE [*suddenly stopping her turning*]: No. I just now thought of something.

JOHN HENRY: You just a little while ago was begging me.

FRANKIE: I know where I'm going.

(*There are sounds of children playing in the distance.*)

JOHN HENRY: Let's go play with the children, Frankie.

FRANKIE: I tell you I know where I'm going. It's like I've known it all my life. Tomorrow I will tell everybody.

JOHN HENRY: Where?

FRANKIE (*dreamily*): After the wedding I'm going with them to Winter Hill. I'm going off with them after the wedding.

JOHN HENRY: You serious?

FRANKIE: Shush, just now I realized something. The trouble with me is that for a long time I have been just an "I" person. All other people can say "we." When Berenice says "we" she means her lodge and church and colored people. Soldiers can say "we" and mean the army. All people belong to a "we" except me.

JOHN HENRY: What are we going to do?

FRANKIE: Not to belong to a "we" makes you too lonesome. Until this afternoon I didn't have a "we," but now after seeing Janice and Jarvis I suddenly realize something.

JOHN HENRY: What?

FRANKIE: I know that the bride and my brother are the "we" of me. So I'm going with them, and joining with the wedding. This coming Sunday when my brother and the bride leave this town, I'm going with the two of them to Winter Hill. And after that to whatever place that they will ever go. (*There is a pause.*) I love the two of them so much and we belong to be together. I love the two of them so much because they are the we of me.

From Carson McCullers, *The Member of the Wedding.* Copyright © 1949, 1951 by Carson McCullers. Reprinted by permission of New Directions Publishing Corporation.

9. With what approaching event is the passage primarily concerned?

(1) a funeral
(2) a picnic
(3) a graduation
(4) a wedding
(5) a dance

10. What is Winter Hill?

(1) the place where Janice and Jarvis plan to live
(2) the place where Frankie lives
(3) the place where the play takes place
(4) the place where John Henry lives
(5) the place where the children are playing

11. By including the noise of children playing in the background, the author emphasizes

(1) that Frankie is still a child

(2) that the children do not like Frankie

(3) that Frankie is leaving childhood behind

(4) that Frankie does not like the children

(5) that John Henry is still just a child

12. With which of the following ideas would Frankie be the LEAST likely to agree?

(1) Three's a crowd.

(2) Family loyalty is important.

(3) A person needs a sense of belonging.

(4) Learning new things is exciting.

(5) Change can come suddenly.

Items 13 to 17 are based on the following passage.

WHAT MAKES AN ACTOR GREAT?

Laurence Olivier at his best is what everyone has ever meant by the phrase "a great actor." He has all the big resources: complete physical relaxation; powerful physical magnetism; commanding eyes that are visible from the back of the gallery; superb timing, which means the capacity to make verse swing, and finally the ability to communicate a sense of danger.

These are all vital attributes, and you can list them in many orders of importance (Olivier himself regards his eyes as his ace of trumps), but the last attribute is surely the rarest. Watching Olivier, you feel that at any moment he may do something utterly unpredictable—something explosive, unnerving in its emotional nakedness. There is nothing bland in this man. He is complex, moody and turbulent. Deep in his temperament there is a vein of rage that his affable public mask cannot wholly conceal. I once asked Ralph Richardson how he differed, as an actor, from Olivier. He replied: "I haven't got Laurence's splendid fury."

Fame, which isolates men from all but their colleagues, has enabled Olivier to preserve into his mid-50's the hair-triggered emotional reactions of adolescence. He has never developed the thick protective social skin beneath which most of us hide our more violent or embarrassing emotions. Within him the volcano remains active, the eruption imminent. This is an actor ruled by instinct, not a rational being or a patient arguer or even a competent chairman. And when you ally this intuitive fire with superb technical machinery and a vast knowledge of audience responses, you have something like the theatrical counterpart of the internal combustion engine.

Out of a sense of duty, Olivier has occasionally tried to play what is insultingly known as "the common man"—the seedy schoolteacher, for instance, in the film *Term of Trial.* He seldom succeeds. That outsize emotional candor cannot help breaking through. The actor bursts the seams of the role and common man becomes exceptional. That is why Olivier has spent the greater part of his professional life with his trousers off—playing bare-legged or in tights the exceptional characters around whom the playwrights of the past built their tallest tragedies and highest comedies.

From "In His Talent, Shakespeare Summoned Up" by Kenneth Tynan. Copyright © 1964 by the author. First appeared in *Life.* Reprinted by permission of Time, Inc.

13. Of all the characteristics that great actors possess, which does the author believe is the rarest?

(1) "complete physical relaxation" (line 4)

(2) "powerful physical magnetism" (lines 4–5)

(3) "commanding eyes" (line 5)

(4) "superb timing" (line 7)

(5) "the ability to communicate a sense of danger" (lines 9-10)

14. The author implies that Olivier is at his best when he is playing

(1) common men
(2) extraordinary men
(3) good men
(4) evil men
(5) quiet men

15. In which of the following productions would the author probably prefer to see Olivier act?

(1) a television comedy
(2) an adventure movie
(3) a light musical
(4) a Shakespeare play
(5) a soap opera

16. What is the author doing when he says that "Olivier himself regards his eyes as his ace of trumps" (lines 13-14)?

(1) He is making a comparison that says that Olivier is proud of his eyes.
(2) He is suggesting that the actor doesn't like his eyes.
(3) He is saying that Olivier likes to play bridge.
(4) He is stating what he thinks is most important.
(5) He is describing the shape of Olivier's eyes.

17. The author compares Olivier to an "internal combustion engine" (line 43) to emphasize

(1) his rough manner
(2) his short temper
(3) his dramatic strength
(4) his smooth movements
(5) his loud voice

Items 18 to 20 are based on the following passage.

HOW DOES NICK FEEL ABOUT DAISY?

Daisy took her face in her hands as if feeling its lovely shape, and her eyes moved gradually out into the velvet dusk. I saw that turbulent emotions possessed her, so I asked what I thought would be some sedative questions about her little girl.

"We don't know each other very well, Nick," she said suddenly. "Even if we are cousins. You didn't come to my wedding."

"I wasn't back from the war."

"That's true." She hesitated. "Well, I've had a very bad time, Nick, and I'm pretty cynical about everything."

Evidently she had reason to be. I waited but she didn't say any more, and after a moment I returned rather feebly to the subject of her daughter.

"I suppose she talks, and—eats, and everything."

"Oh, yes." She looked at me absently. "Listen, Nick; let me tell you what I said when she was born. Would you like to hear?"

"Very much."

"It'll show you how I've gotten to feel about—things. Well, she was less than an hour old and Tom was God knows where. I woke up out of the ether with an utterly abandoned feeling, and asked the nurse right away if it was a boy or a girl. She told me it was a girl, and so I turned my head away and wept. 'All right,' I said, 'I'm glad it's a girl. And I hope she'll be a fool—that's the best thing a girl can be in this world, a beautiful little fool.'

"You see I think everything's terrible anyhow," she went on in a convinced way. "Everybody thinks so—the most advanced people. And I *know*. I've been everywhere and seen everything and done everything." Her eyes flashed around her in a defiant way, rather like Tom's, and she laughed with a thrilling scorn. "Sophisticated—God, I'm sophisticated!"

The instant her voice broke off, ceasing to compel my attention, my belief, I felt the basic insincerity of what she had said. It made me uneasy, as though the whole evening had been a trick of some sort to exact a contributary emotion from me. I waited, and sure enough, in a moment she looked at me with an absolute smirk on her lovely face, as if she had asserted her membership in a rather distinguished secret society to which she and Tom belonged.

From *The Great Gatsby* by F. Scott Fitzgerald. Copyright © 1953 by Frances Scott Fitzgerald Lanahan. Copyright © 1991, 1992 by Eleanor Lanahan, Matthew Bruccoli, and Samuel J. Lanahan as trustees under agreement dated July 3, 1975 created by Frances Scott Fitzgerald Smith. Reprinted by permission of Charles Scribner's Sons.

18. The conversation in this passage takes place between

(1) total strangers
(2) cousins
(3) parent and child
(4) husband and wife
(5) former lovers

19. What does Daisy hope that her daughter will become?

(1) a simple-minded but lovely woman
(2) a wife and mother
(3) a politician
(4) a sophisticated young woman
(5) a musician

20. Daisy's "Sophisticated—God, I'm sophisticated!" (line 45) indicates

(1) she does not want her daughter to follow in her footsteps
(2) she no longer loves her husband
(3) she thinks that Nick isn't good enough for her
(4) she is bored with her life
(5) she is trying to attract Nick

Items 21 to 23 are based on the following poem.

HOW DOES THE AIRMAN FEEL ABOUT HIS FATE?

An Irish Airman Forsees His Death

I know that I shall meet my fate
Somewhere among the clouds above;
Those that I fight I do not hate,
Those that I guard I do not love;
My country is Kiltartan Cross,
My countrymen Kiltartan's poor.
No likely end could bring them loss
Or leave them happier than before.
Nor law, nor duty bade me fight,
Nor public men, nor cheering crowds,
A lonely impulse of delight
Drove to this tumult in the clouds;
I balanced all, brought all to mind,
The years to come seemed waste of breath,
A waste of breath the years behind
In balance with this life, this death.

"An Irish Airman Foresees His Death" by William Butler Yeats. Reprinted with permission of Macmillan Publishing Company from *The Poems of W. B. Yeats: A New Edition* edited by Richard J. Finneran. Copyright © 1919 by Macmillan Publishing Company, renewed 1947 by Bertha Georgie Yeats.

21. What drove the speaker to become a pilot in the war?

(1) a government order
(2) a need for security
(3) a whim
(4) peer pressure
(5) boredom with his civilian job

22. Whom does the speaker seem to care the most about?

(1) the people in Kiltartan Cross
(2) the people of Ireland
(3) himself
(4) his sweetheart
(5) his mother

23. Which of the following words best describes the speaker's emotions?

(1) sarcastic
(2) resigned
(3) hopeful
(4) terrified
(5) angry

Answers are on pages 96–97.

Half-Length Practice Test

Performance Analysis Chart

Directions: Circle the number of each item that you got correct on the Half-Length Practice Test. Count how many items you got correct in each row; count how many items you got correct in each column. Write the amount correct per row and column as the numerator in the fraction in the appropriate "Total Correct" box. (The denominators represent the total number of items in the row or column.) Write the grand total correct over the denominator, **23**, at the lower right corner of the chart. (For example, if you got 20 items correct, write *20* so that the fraction reads 20/**23**.)

Item Type	Nonfiction (page 1)	Fiction (page 10)	Drama (page 19)	Poetry (page 28)	Commentary (page 38)	TOTAL CORRECT
Literal Comprehension		1, 18, 19	9	21	13	**/6**
Inferential Comprehension	5, 6, 7	2, 20	10	22	14	**/8**
Application		3	12		15	**/3**
Analysis	8	4	11	23	16, 17	**/6**
TOTAL CORRECT	**/4**	**/7**	**/4**	**/3**	**/5**	**/23**

The page numbers in parentheses indicate where in this book you can find more exercises of the various types of literature and commentary and the types of questions you encountered on the Practice Test.

Full-length Practice Test

Directions: Choose the one best answer for each question.

Items 1 to 4 are based on the following passage.

WHY DOES BALTHAZAR GIVE HIS CAGE AWAY?

Balthazar was no stranger to José Montiel's house. On different occasions, because of his skill and his forthright way of dealing, he had been called in to do minor carpentry jobs. But he never felt at ease among the rich. He used to think about them, about their ugly and argumentative wives, about their tremendous surgical operations, and he always experienced a feeling of pity. When he entered their houses, he couldn't move without dragging his feet....

José Montiel, obese and hairy, his towel draped around his neck, appeared at the bedroom window.

"What is that?"

"Pepe's cage," said Balthazar.

His wife looked at him perplexedly.

"Whose?"

"Pepe's" replied Balthazar. And then, turning toward José Montiel, "Pepe ordered it."...

Pepe appeared in the doorway. He was about twelve, and had the same curved eyelashes and was as quietly pathetic as his mother.

"Come here," José Montiel said to him. "Did you order this?"

The child lowered his head. Grabbing him by the hair, José Montiel forced Pepe to look him in the eye.

"Answer me."

The child bit his lip without replying.,

"Montiel," whispered his wife.

José Montiel let the child go and turned toward Balthazar in a fury. "I'm very sorry, Balthazar," he said. "But you should have consulted me before going on. Only to you would it occur to contract with a minor." As he spoke, his face recovered its serenity. He lifted the cage without looking at it and gave it to Balthazar...

"Pepe," said Balthazar.

He approached the child, smiling, and held the cage out to him. The child jumped up, embraced the cage which was almost as big as he was, and stood looking at Balthazar through the wirework without knowing what to say....

"Don't be foolish, Balthazar," he was saying, blocking his path. "Take your piece of furniture home and don't be silly. I have no intention of paying you a cent."

"It doesn't matter," said Balthazar. "I made it expressly as a gift for Pepe. I didn't expect to charge anything for it."

As Balthazar made his way through the spectators who were blocking the door, José Montiel was shouting in the middle of the living room. He was very pale and his eyes were beginning to get red.

"Idiot!" he was shouting. "Take your trinket out of here. The last thing we need is for some nobody to give orders in my house. Son of a bitch!"

From "Balthazar's Marvelous Afternoon" by Gabriel Garcia Marquez. Copyright © 1968 in the English translation by Harper & Row. Reprinted by permission.

1. Which of the following best describes José Montiel?

(1) compassionate but firm
(2) clever and thoughtful
(3) egotistical but friendly
(4) short-tempered and cruel
(5) foolish and careless

2. Where does this scene take place?

(1) at a local tavern
(2) at the home of Balthazar
(3) at the home of José Montiel
(4) at Balthazar's shop
(5) at an outdoor market

3. Why does José Montiel become angry with Balthazar?

(1) Balthazar has made him lose his temper with his son.
(2) He feels that Balthazar refuses to recognize his authority.
(3) Balthazar expects to be paid for work that was commissioned by a twelve-year-old.
(4) He feels that Balthazar has overcharged him for the cage.
(5) He fears that Balthazar is trying to cheat him again.

4. Based on the one sentence in which Montiel's wife is mentioned, it can be inferred that she

(1) agrees with Montiel
(2) is angry
(3) wants to avoid the upcoming scene
(4) is defending her son
(5) feels that Balthazar is right

5. How will Balthazar probably react the next time he is asked to visit a wealthy home?

(1) He will turn down the job; this experience has frightened him badly.
(2) He will hesitate; this time, he will get a written contract before he does any work.
(3) He will be fearful; he will worry that he will anger his client again.
(4) He will feel more comfortable; he has seen that rich people are not automatically superior.
(5) He will accept the job humbly; he will feel he acted badly in his confrontation with Montiel.

Items 6 to 9 are based on the following passage.

WHO WAS THE AUTHOR'S FIRST MOVIE HERO?

In the summer of 1943 I was eight, and my father and mother and small brother and I were at Peterson Field in Colorado Springs. A hot wind blew through that summer, blew until it seemed that before August broke, all the dust in Kansas would be in Colorado, would have drifted over the tar-paper barracks and the temporary strip and stopped only when it hit Pikes Peak. There was not much to do, a summer like that: there was the day they brought in the first B-29, an event to remember but scarcely a vacation program. There was an Officers' Club, but no swimming pool; all the Officers' Club had of interest was artificial blue rain behind the bar. The rain interested me a good deal, but I could not spend the summer watching it, and so we went, my brother and I, to the movies.

We went three and four afternoons a week, sat on folding chairs in the darkened Quonset hut which served as a theater, and it was there, that summer of 1943 while the hot wind blew outside, that I first saw John Wayne. Saw the walk, heard the voice. Heard him tell a girl in a picture called *War of the Wildcats* that he would build her a house, "at the bend in the river where the cottonwoods grow." As it happened I did not grow up to be the kind of woman who is the heroine in a Western, and although the men I have known have had many virtues and have taken me to live in many places I have come to love, they have never been John Wayne, and they have never taken me to that bend in the river where the cottonwoods grow. Deep in that part of my heart where the artificial rain falls forever, that is still the line I wait to hear.

Reprinted by permission of Farrar, Straus and Giroux, Inc. Excerpt from "John Wayne: A Love Song" from *Slouching Toward Bethlehem* by Joan Didion. Copyright © 1965, 1968 by Joan Didion.

6. How often did the author go to the movies in the summer of 1943?

(1) once a week
(2) one to two times a week
(3) three to four times a week
(4) once a month
(5) every day

7. What was it about John Wayne that attracted the author?

(1) his physical strength
(2) his rugged good looks
(3) the way he walked
(4) his brilliant portrayals of different kinds of characters
(5) the romantic quality of his characters

8. What advice would the author probably give to a young girl who has a crush on a rock star?

(1) "Cherish these feelings, but look for happiness in the real world, too."
(2) "You're too young to be concerned about such things."
(3) "If you wait long enough, your dreams will come true."
(4) "Real life is better than romantic fantasies."
(5) "Work to make your dreams come true."

9. When she refers to "that part of my heart where the artificial rain falls forever (lines 40-41)," the author uses the artificial rain to represent

(1) her broken dreams
(2) her childhood fantasies
(3) beauty
(4) freedom
(5) the pain of growing old

Items 10 to 13 are based on the following passage.

WHAT DO GEORGE AND LENNIE WANT?

LENNIE (*craftily*): Tell me—like you done before.

GEORGE: Tell you what?

LENNIE: About the rabbits.

GEORGE (*near to anger again*): You ain't gonna put nothing over on me!

LENNIE (*pleading*): Come on, George... tell me! Please! Like you done before.

GEORGE: You get a kick out of that, don't you? All right, I'll tell you. And then we'll lay out our beds and eat our dinner.

LENNIE: Go on, George. (*Unrolls his bed and lies on his side, supporting his head on one hand. George lays out his bed and sits cross-legged on it. George repeats the next speech rhythmically, as though he had said it many times before.*)

GEORGE: Guys like up that work on ranches is the loneliest guys in the world. They ain't got no family. They don't belong no place. They come to a ranch and work up a stake and they go in to town and blow their stake. And then the first thing you know they're poundin' their tail on some other ranch. They ain't got nothing to look ahead to.

LENNIE (*delightedly*): That's it, that's it! Now tell how it is with us.

GEORGE (*still almost chanting*): With us it ain't like that. We got a future. We got somebody to talk to that gives a damn about us. We don't have to sit in no barroom blowin' in our jack, just because we got no place else to go. If them other guys gets in jail, they can rot for all anybody gives a damn.

LENNIE (*who cannot restrain himself any longer. Bursts into speech.*): But not us! And why? Because... because

I got you to look after me... and you got me to look after you... and that's why! (*He laughs.*) Go on, George!

GEORGE: You got it by heart. You can do it yourself.

LENNIE: No, tell how it's gonna be!

GEORGE: Okay. Some day we're gonna get the jack together and we're gonna have a little house, and a couple of acres and a cow and some pigs and...

LENNIE (*shouting*): And live off the fat of the land! And have rabbits. Go on, George! Tell about what we're gonna have in the garden. And about the rabbits in the cages. Tell about the rain in the winter... and about the stove and how thick the cream is on the milk, you can hardly cut it. Tell about that, George!

From *Of Mice and Men* by John Steinbeck. Copyright © 1937 by the author. Reprinted by permission of Viking Penguin, Inc.

10. The information in the passage indicates that Lennie and George

(1) have just met
(2) travel around together
(3) are enemies
(4) are brothers
(5) grew up together

11. What is the topic of George and Lennie's conversation?

(1) rabbits
(2) the criminal activities of their friends
(3) the difficulties of life on a ranch
(4) their dreams for a more settled future
(5) spending time in bars

12. By including dialogue in which Lennie keeps interrupting George's story, the playwright encourages the audience

(1) to pity George for the burden of his friendship
(2) to laugh at Lennie's childishness
(3) to feel sympathy for Lennie and his enthusiasm
(4) to anticipate how the scene will end
(5) to suspect both George and Lennie

13. According to George, what is wrong with the lives of hired ranch hands?

(1) They can't raise rabbits.
(2) They drink too much.
(3) They have to work too hard.
(4) Their wages are too low.
(5) They have no permanent home.

Items 14 to 18 are based on the following passage.

WHICH ARE THE BEST FILM COMEDIES?

In the language of screen comedians four of the main grades of laugh are the titter, the yowl, the bellylaugh and the boffo. The titter is just a titter. The yowl is a runaway titter. Anyone who has ever had the pleasure knows all about a belly-laugh. The boffo is the laugh that kills. An ideally good gag, perfectly constructed and played, would bring the victim up this ladder of laughs by cruelly controlled degrees to the top rung, and would then proceed to wobble, shake, wave and brandish the ladder until he groaned for mercy. Then, after the shortest possible time out for recuperation, he would feel the first wicked tickling of the comedian's whip once more and start up a new ladder.

The reader can get a fair enough idea of the current state of screen comedy by asking himself how long it has been since he has had that treatment. The best of comedies these days hand out plenty of titters and once in a while it is possible to achieve a yowl without overstraining. Even those who have never seen anything better must occasionally have the feeling, as they watch the current run or, rather, trickle of screen comedy, that they are having to make a little cause for laughter go an awfully long way. And anyone who has watched screen comedy over the past ten or fifteen years is bound to realize that it has quietly but steadily deteriorated. As for those happy atavists who remember silent comedy in its heyday and the bellylaughs and boffos that went with it, they have something close to an absolute standard by which to measure the deterioration.

When a modern comedian gets hit on the head, for example, the most he is apt to do is look sleepy. When a silent comedian got hit on the head he seldom let it go so flatly. He realized a broad license, and a ruthless discipline within that license. It was his business to be as funny as possible physically, without the help or hindrance of words. So he gave us a figure of speech, or rather a vision, for loss of consciousness. In other words he gave us a poem, a kind of poem, moreover, that everybody understands. The least he might do was to straighten up stiff as a plank and fall over backward with such skill that his whole length seemed to slap the floor at the same instant. Or he might make a cadenza of it—look vague, smile like an angel, roll up his eyes, lace his fingers, thrust his hands palms downward as far as they would go, hunch his shoulders, rise on tiptoe, prance ecstatically in narrowing circles until, with tallow knees, he sank down the vortex of his dizziness to the floor, and there signified nirvana by kicking his heels twice, like a swimming frog.

From "Comedy's Greatest Era" by James Agee reprinted by permission of Grosset & Dunlap from Agee on Film, Vol. 1 copyright © 1958 by The James Agee Trust, copyright renewed © 1986 by Teresa, Andrea and John Agee.

14. According to the author, modern screen comedies are

(1) funnier than silent screen comedies
(2) more expensive to make than silent screen comedies
(3) more sophisticated than silent screen comedies
(4) larger than silent screen comedies
(5) less funny than silent screen comedies

15. Which of the following sight gags does the author use to compare kinds of comedians?

(1) a funny walk
(2) slipping on a banana peel
(3) reacting to a hit on the head
(4) car chases
(5) a cream pie

16. Which of the following would the author probably prefer to watch on TV?

(1) a talk show
(2) a situation comedy with humorous dialogue
(3) a situation comedy with sight gags
(4) a news broadcast
(5) a live broadcast of a symphony performance

17. Why does the author begin the passage by describing the four main grades of laughter?

(1) to show how much he knows about comedy
(2) to show how simple it is to make people laugh
(3) to emphasize which kind of laughter is best
(4) to show the kinds of laughter good comedy can produce
(5) to give the reader the technical names for different laughs

18. By using the image of a "comedian's whip" and "ladder" (lines 9-18), the author demonstrates the comedian's

(1) use of violence to make people laugh
(2) control of the audience's emotions
(3) ability to make a lot of noise
(4) attraction to violence
(5) hidden cruelty

Items 19 to 22 are based on the following poem.

WHAT IS THE SPEAKER'S ATTITUDE TOWARD THE CLARINET PLAYER?

For Free

I slept last night in a good hotel
I went shopping today for jewels
The wind rushed around in the dirty town
And the children let out from the schools
I was standing on a noisy corner
Waiting for the walking green
Across the street he stood
And he played real good
On his clarinet, for free.

Now me I play for fortune
And those velvet curtain calls
I've got a black limousine
And two gentlemen
Escorting me to the halls

And I play if you have the money
Or if you're a friend to me
But the one man band
By the quick lunch stand
He was playing real good, for free.

Nobody stopped to hear him
Though he played so sweet and high
They knew he had never
Been on their T.V.
So they passed his music by
I meant to go over and ask for a song
Maybe put on a harmony...
I heard his refrain
As the signal changed
He was playing real good, for free.

"For Free" by Joni Mitchell. © 1970, 1974 Siquomb Publishing Corp. All rights reserved. Used by permission.

19. According to the poem, where is the clarinet player performing?

(1) in a hotel
(2) at a concert hall
(3) in a living room
(4) in the street
(5) at a supermarket

20. The first two lines of stanza 2 imply that the speaker is

(1) a successful musician
(2) a rich stockbroker
(3) a well-known actress
(4) a lucky gambler
(5) a critically-acclaimed dancer

21. Why does the poet repeat three times that the clarinet player was performing "for free"?

(1) to indicate that the clarinet player is not very smart
(2) to reveal that the clarinet player is performing for a charity
(3) to stress the contrast between the clarinet player and the speaker
(4) to emphasize that the clarinet player is a wonderful person
(5) to show that the clarinet player is not very good

22. Why didn't anyone stop to listen to the street musician?

(1) People are in too much of a hurry.
(2) Clarinet music is not very popular.
(3) He wasn't anyone famous.
(4) His music couldn't be heard over the noise of the city.
(5) People were afraid he would ask for money.

Items 23 to 26 are based on the following passage.

WHAT DOES FIRST LOVE FEEL LIKE?

My heart was pounding, and I didn't know why. I hadn't known I could feel like this—that I could pause on the edge of such feeling, which lay stretched like an enormous meadow all in shadow inside me. It seemed to me a miracle that human beings could be so elaborate. "Listen, Eleanor," I said, "you're all right! I've *always* liked you." I swallowed and moved closer to her; there were two moist streaks running down her face. I raised my arm and, with the sleeve of my shirt, I wiped away her tears. "I think you're wonderful! I think you're really something!"

"You look down on me," she said. "I know you do. I can tell."

"How can I, Eleanor? How *can* I?" I cried. "I'm nobody. I've been damaged by my heredity."

"You, too!" she exclaimed happily. "Oh, that's what's wrong with me!"

A sudden hiss swept through the air and then the first raindrops struck the street. "Quick!" Eleanor cried, and we ran up on her porch. Two bursts of lightning lit up the dark sky, and the rain streamed down. I held Eleanor's hand, and we stood watching the rain. "It's a real thundershower," she said.

"Do you feel bad because we only started being friends tonight? I mean, do you feel you're on the rebound and settling on the second-best?" I asked. There was a long silence and all around it was the sound of the rain.

"I don't think so," Eleanor said at last. "How about you?"

I raised my eye brows and said, "Oh, no, it doesn't bother me at all."

"That's good," she said.

We were standing very close to one another. We talked industriously. "I don't like geometry," Eleanor said. "I don't see what use it is. It's supposed to train your mind, but I don't believe it... ."

I took my glasses off. "Eleanor—" I said. I kissed her, passionately, and then I turned away, pounding my fists on top of each other. "Excuse me," I whispered hoarsely. That kiss had lasted a long time, and I thought I would die.

Excerpt from *First Love and Other Sorrows* by Harold Brodkey. Copyright © 1954, 1955, 1957 by the author. Reprinted by permission of Random House, Inc.

23. Eleanor's responses to the narrator in lines 16-17 indicate that she feels

(1) he is too experienced to take her seriously
(2) she is older than he is and cannot take him seriously
(3) she is unworthy of his love
(4) he is unworthy of her love
(5) he does not respect her enough

24. The two characters in the excerpt could best be described as

(1) frightened and depressed
(2) happy but insecure
(3) happy and carefree
(4) nervous and angry
(5) excited but angry

25. With which of the following statements would the narrator most likely agree?

(1) Wonder and pain combine in moments of intense happiness.
(2) Happiness begins to die down as soon as it hits a peak.
(3) Self-doubt can destroy the most positive experience.
(4) Human beings cannot communicate their strongest emotions.
(5) Young love is a storm that causes more pain than joy.

26. Eleanor talks about geometry in lines 43-46 probably

(1) to make the narrator think she is intelligent

(2) to convince the narrator she does not feel he is "second best"

(3) to take his mind off the thunderstorm

(4) to reduce tension about their new intimacy

(5) to indicate that she is not really attracted to him

Items 27 to 30 are based on the following passage.

CAN ELWOOD REALLY SEE A GIANT WHITE RABBIT?

ELWOOD: I had just helped Ed Hickey into a taxi. Ed had been mixing his rye with his gin, and I felt he needed conveying. I started to walk down the street when I heard a voice saying: "Good evening, Mr. Dowd." I turned and there was this great white rabbit leaning against a lamp-post. Well, I thought nothing of that, because when you have lived in a town as long as I have lived in this one, you get used to the fact that everybody knows your name. Naturally, I went over to chat with him. He said to me: "Ed Hickey is a little spiffed this evening, or could I be mistaken?" Well, of course he was not mistaken. I think the world and all of Ed but he was spiffed. Well, anyway, we stood there and talked, and finally I said,—"You have the advantage of me. You know my name and I don't know yours." Right back at me he said: "What name do you like?" Well, I didn't even have to think a minute: Harvey has always been my favorite name. So I said, "Harvey," and this is the interesting part of the whole thing. He said—"What a coincidence! My name happens to be Harvey."

SANDERSON (*crossing above desk*): What was your father's name, Dowd?

ELWOOD: John. John Frederick.

SANDERSON: Dowd, when you were a child you had a playmate, didn't you? Someone you were very fond of—with whom you spent many happy, carefree hours?

ELWOOD: Oh, yes, Doctor. Didn't you?

SANDERSON: What was his name?

ELWOOD: Verne. Verne McElhinney. Did you ever know the McElhinneys, Doctor?

SANDERSON: No.

ELWOOD: Too bad. There were a lot of them, and they circulated. Wonderful people.

SANDERSON: Think carefully, Dowd. Wasn't there someone, somewhere, some time, whom you knew—by the name of Harvey? Didn't you ever know anybody by that name?

ELWOOD: No, Doctor. No one. Maybe that's why I always had such hopes for it.

From *Harvey* by Mary Chase. Copyright © 1943 by Mary Chase (under the title *The White Rabbit)* Copyright © 1944 by Mary Chase (under the title *Harvey)* Renewed 1970, 1971. Caution: the reprinting of *Harvey* is by permission of the owners and Dramatists Play Service, Inc. The amateur performance rights are controlled exclusively by Dramatists Play Service, Inc. No amateur performance may be given without obtaining, in advance, the written permission of Dramatists Play Service, Inc. and paying the requisite fee. Inquiries on stock production should be addressed to Robert A. Freedman Dramatic Agency, Inc.

27. According to Elwood, what did Harvey see Elwood do before he started their first conversation?

(1) get into an argument with his father

(2) lean against a lamp-post

(3) come out of a bar

(4) help Ed Hickey get into a taxicab

(5) play with Verne McElhinney

28. Dr. Sanderson's questions to Elwood suggest that he

(1) is interested in Elwood's family
(2) is jealous of Elwood's friend
(3) does not believe Elwood's story
(4) wants to find out where Harvey came from
(5) wishes that he had had a happy, carefree childhood

29. What is the most likely reason for Elwood's conversation with Dr. Sanderson?

(1) Elwood is worried about Ed Hickey's drinking.
(2) Harvey isn't feeling very well.
(3) Elwood believes he is losing his mind.
(4) Someone who was worried about Elwood's mental health referred him to the doctor.
(5) Dr. Sanderson is interviewing people who own white rabbits.

30. The playwright achieves humor in this passage by all of the following EXCEPT

(1) by showing Dr. Sanderson's frustration
(2) by making the topic of the conversation ridiculous
(3) by having Elwood speak to Harvey in Dr. Sanderson's presence
(4) by having Elwood tell his story in a very matter-of-fact way
(5) by having Elwood explain why he had high hopes for the name Harvey

Items 31 to 35 are based on the following passage.

WHAT MADE THE TOWN DUMP SUCH AN INTERESTING PLACE?

The town dump of Whitemud, Saskatchewan, could only have been a few years old when I knew it, for the village was born in 1913 and I left there in 1919. But I remember the dump better than I remember most things in that town, better than I remember most of the people. I spent more time with it, for one thing; it has more poetry and excitement in it than people did.

It lays in the southeast corner of town, in a section that was always full of adventure for me. Just there the Whitemud River left the hills, bent a little south, and started its long traverse across the prairie and international boundary to join the Milk. For all I knew, it might have been on its way to join the Alph: Simply, before my eyes, it disappeared into a strangeness and wonder.

Also, where it passed below the dumpground, it ran through willowed bottoms that were a favorite campsite for passing teamsters, gypsies, sometimes Indians. The very straw scattered around those camps, the ashes of those strangers' campfires, the manure of their teams and saddle horses, were hot with adventurous possibilities.

It was as an extension, a living suburb, as it were, of the dumpground that we most valued those camps. We scoured them for artifacts of their migrant tenants as if they had been archaeological sites full of the secrets of ancient civilizations. I remember toting around for weeks the broken cheek strap of a bridle. Somehow or other its buckle looked as if it had been fashioned in a far place, a place where they were accustomed to flatten the tongues of buckles for reasons that could only be exciting, and where they made a habit of plating the metal with some valuable alloy, probably silver. In places where the silver was worn away the buckle underneath shone dull yellow: probably gold.

From "The Town Dump" by Wallace Stegner. Originally appeared in the *Atlantic Monthly* in October 1959. Copyright © 1955, 1957, 1959, 1959, 1962 by the author. Reprinted by permission of Brandt & Brandt Literary Agents.

31. Where was the town dump?

(1) in the middle of Whitemud
(2) across the prairie
(3) on the Alph River
(4) near a campsite for travelers
(5) north of town

32. According to the information in the passage, the term "migrant" means

(1) wandering
(2) dangerous
(3) poor
(4) adventurous
(5) ragged

33. What conclusion can you make about the author's age when he lived in Whitemud?

(1) he was a middle-aged man
(2) he was a teenager
(3) he was a child
(4) he was a young adult
(5) he was an old man

34. Which of the following phrases would the author most likely choose to suggest how he once felt about the dump?

(1) a frightening country
(2) a magic kingdom
(3) a lonely frontier
(4) a depressing playground
(5) an empty campground

35. To emphasize that the camps were like "archaeological sites" (paragraph four), the author uses which of the following words?

(1) suburb
(2) buckle
(3) gold
(4) dumpground
(5) artifacts

Items 36 to 39 are based on the following poem.

WHAT DOES THE PASSAGE OF TIME LEAVE US?

Break, Break, Break

Break, break, break,
On thy cold gray stones, O Sea!
And I would that my tongue could utter
The thoughts that arise in me.

O, well for the fisherman's boy,
that he shouts with his sister at play!
O, well for the sailor lad,
That he sings in his boat on the bay!

And the stately ships go on
To their haven under the hill;
But O for the touch of a vanished hand,
And the sound of a voice that is still!

Break, break, break,
At the foot of thy crags, O Sea!
But the tender grace of a day that is dead
Will never come back to me.

"Break, Break, Break" by Alfred Lord Tennyson

36. Most of the images in the poem are concerned with

(1) music
(2) stones
(3) the sky
(4) mountains
(5) the ocean

37. In lines 11–12, the speaker is talking about

(1) someone he knew who moved away
(2) someone who is sitting quietly next to him
(3) someone he never actually met
(4) someone he knew who died
(5) someone he read about in a book

38. The line "Break, break, break" (lines 1 and 13) is intended

(1) to emphasize the cruelty of the ocean

(2) to imitate the pounding of the surf

(3) to symbolize the finality of death

(4) to symbolize life in its many varieties

(5) to reveal the poet's expectation of his own death

39. Why does the poet use "O" five times in this short poem?

(1) to make it seem longer

(2) to emphasize the idea of exclamation

(3) to create a round sound

(4) to emphasize the sadness of the poem

(5) to set up a contrast with the sea

Items 40 to 45 are based on the following passage.

WHAT CAN A WORK OF ART REVEAL ABOUT ITS CREATOR?

"Where I was born and where and how I have lived is unimportant," Georgia O'Keeffe told us in the book of paintings and words published in her ninetieth year on earth. She seemed to be advising us to forget the beautiful face in the Stieglitz photographs. She appeared to be dismissing the rather condescending romance that had attached to her by then, the romance of extreme good looks and advanced age and deliberate isolation. "It is what I have done with where I have been that should be of interest." I recall an August afternoon in Chicago in 1973 when I took my daughter, then seven, to see what Georgia O'Keeffe had done with where she had been. One of the vast O'Keeffe "Sky Above Clouds" canvases floated over the back stairs in the Chicago Art Institute that day, dominating what seemed to be several stories of empty light, and my daughter looked at it once, ran to the landing, and kept on looking. "Who drew it," she whispered after a while. I told her. "I need to talk to her," she said finally.

My daughter was making, that day in Chicago, an entirely unconscious but quite basic assumption about people and the work they do. She was assuming that the glory she saw in the work reflected a glory in its maker, that the painting was the painter as the poem is the poet, that every choice one made alone—every word chosen or rejected, every brush stroke laid or not laid down—betrayed one's character. *Style is character*. It seemed to me that afternoon that I had rarely seen so instinctive an application of this familiar principle, and I recall being pleased not only that my daughter responded to style as character but that it was Georgia O'Keeffe's particular style to which she responded: this was a hard woman who had imposed her 192 square feet of clouds on Chicago.

From *The White Album* by Joan Didion. Copyright © 1979 by the author. Reprinted by permission of Simon & Schuster.

40. Which phrase best captures the main idea of the passage?

(1) children make the best critics

(2) big paintings are often better

(3) landscape is the best subject for art

(4) style often reflects character

(5) hard people make the best artists

41. From the information in the first paragraph, it can be concluded that Georgia O'Keeffe

(1) is known for her interesting life as well as for her art

(2) was actually an uninteresting person

(3) is best known as a photographer

(4) wanted to be remembered as a colorful oddball

(5) was a personal friend of the author

42. As it is used in the passage (paragraph two), the word "betrayed" most nearly means

(1) emphasized
(2) revealed
(3) concealed
(4) illustrated
(5) ruined

43. According to the author, if you listened to many works of music by the same composer you would probably

(1) learn to recognize the composer's style
(2) learn something about the composer's personality
(3) grow tired of the composer's music
(4) grow to understand the composer's music
(5) learn something about the composer's nationality

44. By using the word "floated" to describe O'Keeffe's painting, "Sky Above Clouds," the author is able to illustrate

(1) how high the painting hangs on the museum's wall
(2) how hard it is to see the painting from the stairs
(3) how well the painting captures a sense of the sky
(4) how light the canvas is on which the painting was painted
(5) how empty of content the painting is despite its size

45. How does the author emphasize the great size of O'Keeffe's "Sky Above Clouds"?

(1) by describing her daughter's reaction to the painting
(2) by explaining that the painting hangs over the stairs
(3) by including the title of the painting
(4) by revealing that the painting hangs in the Art Institute of Chicago
(5) by giving the painting's dimensions in square feet

Answers are on pages 97–101.

Full-Length Practice Test

Performance Analysis Chart

Directions: Circle the number of each item that you got correct on the Full-Length Practice Test. Count how many items you got correct in each row; count how many items you got correct in each column. Write the amount correct per row and column as the numerator in the fraction in the appropriate "Total Correct" box. (The denominators represent the total number of items in the row or column.) Write the grand total correct over the denominator, **45**, at the lower right corner of the chart. (For example, if you got 40 items correct, write *40* so that the fraction reads 40/**45.**)

Item Type	Nonfiction (page 1)	Fiction (page 10)	Drama (page 19)	Poetry (page 28)	Commentary (page 38)	TOTAL CORRECT
Literal Comprehension	6, 31, 32	2, 23	11, 13, 27	19, 22, 36	14, 15, 40	**/14**
Inferential Comprehension	7, 33	1, 3, 4, 24	10, 28, 29	20, 37	41, 42	**/13**
Application	8, 34	5, 25			16, 43	**/6**
Analysis	9, 35	26	12,30	21, 38, 39	17,18 44, 45	**/12**
TOTAL CORRECT	**/9**	**/9**	**/8**	**/8**	**/11**	**/45**

The page numbers in parentheses indicate where in this book you can find more exercises of the various types of literature and commentary and the types of questions you encountered on the Practice Test.

Simulated Test

Directions: Choose the one best answer for each question.

Items 1 to 4 are based on the following passage.

WHAT HAPPENS TO WALTER MITTY IN WATERBURY?

When he came out into the street again, with the overshoes in a box under his arm, Walter Mitty began to wonder what the other thing was his wife had told him to get. She had told him twice, before they set out from their house for Waterbury. In a way he hated these weekly trips to town—he was always getting something wrong. Kleenex, he thought, Squibb's razor blades? No. Toothpaste, toothbrush, bicarbonate, carborundum, initiative and referendum? He gave it up. But she would remember it. "Where's the what's-its-name?" she would ask. "Don't tell me you forgot the what's-its-name." A newsboy went by shouting something about the Waterbury trial.

..."Perhaps this will refresh your memory." The District Attorney suddenly thrust a heavy automatic at the quiet figure on the witness stand. "Have you ever seen this before?" Walter Mitty took the gun and examined it expertly. "This is my Webley-Vickers 50.80," he said calmly. An excited buzz ran around the courtroom. The judge rapped for order. "You are a crack shot with any sort of firearms, I believe?" said the District Attorney, insinuatingly. "Objection!" shouted Mitty's attorney. "We have shown that the defendant could not have fired the shot. We have shown that he wore his right arm in a sling on the night of the fourteenth of July." Walter Mitty raised his hand briefly and the bickering attorneys were stilled. "With any known make of gun," he said evenly, "I could have killed Gregory Fitzhurst at three hundred feet with my left hand" Pandemonium broke loose in the courtroom. A woman's scream rose above the bedlam and suddenly a lovely, dark-haired girl was in Walter Mitty's arms. The District Attorney struck at her savagely. Without rising from his chair, Mitty let the man have it on the point of the chin. "You miserable cur!"....

"Puppy biscuit," said Walter Mitty. He stopped walking and the buildings of Waterbury rose up out of the misty courtroom and surrounded him again. A woman who was passing laughed. "He said 'Puppy biscuit,'" she said to her companion. "That man said 'Puppy biscuit' to himself." Walter Mitty hurried on. He went into an A&P, not the first one he came to but a smaller one farther up the street. "I want some biscuit for small, young dogs," he said to the clerk. "Any special brand, sir?" The greatest pistol shot in the world thought for a moment. "It says 'Puppies Bark for It' on the box," said Walter Mitty.

From "The Secret Life of Walter Mitty" by James Thurber. Copyright © 1942 James Thurber. Copyright ©1970 Helen Thurber and Rosemary A. Thurber. From My World—and Welcome To It, published by Harcourt Brace Jovanovich.

1. What is Walter Mitty doing in Waterbury?
   (1) buying a car
   (2) seeing a doctor
   (3) getting some lunch
   (4) going to court
   (5) doing some errands

2. It can be assumed that the action in the second paragraph (lines 17-43) takes place
   (1) on television
   (2) in Walter Mitty's mind
   (3) in Walter Mitty's real life
   (4) in another town
   (5) in Walter Mitty's novel

3. Walter Mitty might be expected to do all of the following EXCEPT

(1) pass a sports car and imagine himself the winner of the Indianapolis 500

(2) go shopping for milk and come back with potato chips

(3) smell smoke and think that he is a fire chief

(4) hear about a tragic accident and immediately forget about it

(5) hear a street musician and dream that he receives a standing ovation at Carnegie Hall

4. The humor in this passage arises primarily from

(1) the contrast between Walter Mitty's dream world and real world

(2) the contrast between Walter Mitty and his wife

(3) the physical description of Mrs. Mitty

(4) the description of Walter Mitty's actions on the witness stand

(5) the surprise that concludes the passage

Items 5 to 9 are based on the following passage.

WHAT GIVES THIS MAN HIS ENERGY?

Stretch is tall and lean. He's about fifty years old, but he looks no older than thirty-five. He has been warned by the doctors not to drink or smoke anymore because he has a heart condition which twice required open-heart surgery. Stretch just laughs at the doctors and their advice. He says that he might as well not live if he's not enjoying life, and life without any liquor or cigarettes "is a lot like being dead anyhow." What they're trying to do is rush him into heaven, he says, and he's not "gonna go for that trip."

He will tell anyone who'll listen that the doctors don't know anything about when somebody's going to die or what smoking cigarettes is going to do to him. He says they've been telling him that he's going to die from smoking and drinking for six or seven years, and he's still going strong. "They was tellin' Winston Churchill the same story for twenty years. They tell everybody that, and they know that eventually everybody's gonna die, and the drinkin' and the cigarettes have nothin' to do with it." But, he says, the doctors can always point and say, Yeah, you see, I told you that dude was goin' die.

According to Stretch, "They gotta be right because everybody's goin' die one day."

Stretch doesn't act like a person with a serious heart condition. He smokes those strong cigarettes with no filters, and you'll see him go to the bar across the street three or four times a day and stay for about fifteen minutes. He may have two or three or more drinks, but he never gets drunk.

He's got an enormous amount of energy for a man of his age in his condition, or in what he says is his doctor's "made-up condition." He's always doing strenuous jobs, carrying heavy boards and equipment. And he's always running back and forth from his car to the shop, across the street, upstairs and downstairs. On top of all that, he lives on the sixth floor, and he runs up and down at least five or six times a day.

Stretch has to wear very soft shoes with crepe on the outside and a cushion on the inside. They are custom-made because Stretch has what must be the worst feet in all of New York City. When he has his special shoes on, he walks with his head tilted way back and moving in a big stride, like a tall drunk leaning way back because he's afraid that if he tries to straighten up he'll topple over forward. But it has nothing to do with being drunk. It's just the comfortable way for him to walk.

But when he doesn't have his special shoes, he has to walk very slowly. He takes about one step a minute, or every thirty seconds at most, like somebody barefoot trying to walk over a spot where he knows there's broken glass but he can't see it. He's also careful not to step on headless paper matches. He tells the Hamites that his feet got so sensitive "from standin' on too many corners."

Stretch was in the Army during World War II, and he says, "All that marchin' wasn't good for me, and they never had shoes that could fit me." Stretch wears something like a size 15.

According to Stretch, he has had all kinds of money problems because of his feet. He says that there was a time when all of his money went into his feet. He says that one year he thinks he spent more money on his feet than he made. Stretch says that sometimes his feet ache so much that he's tempted to rob a bank to get some money to solve the problem.

From Claude Brown, "Stretch," in The Children of Ham, copyright 1973, 1976 by Claude Brown. Reprinted by permission.

5. Which of the following is NOT described in this passage?

(1) Stretch's physical condition
(2) Stretch's attitude toward doctors
(3) what kind of business Stretch is in
(4) what Stretch might do in a day
(5) the way Stretch walks

6. What does Stretch do against the doctors' advice?

(1) work too hard
(2) walk a lot
(3) drive a car
(4) smoke and drink
(5) wear special shoes

7. Why does Stretch talk about Winston Churchill?

(1) to prove that doctors are always right
(2) to prove that everyone is going to die
(3) to cite a famous person who also drank and smoked
(4) to impress his listeners with his knowledge
(5) to explain why he has lived so long

8. Why does the author provide details about Stretch's foot problem?

(1) because the author is a doctor
(2) because they explain why Stretch robbed a bank
(3) to criticize the Army
(4) to get the reader's sympathy
(5) to emphasize how little Stretch lets problems get in his way

9. Based on the passage, which of the following would Stretch be LEAST likely to do after a hard day's work?

(1) complain about his aching back
(2) tell a joke about his day
(3) have a couple of drinks
(4) go out on a quick errand
(5) carry a heavy load upstairs

Items 10 to 15 are based on the following passage.

IS SEIZE THE DAY AS GOOD A FILM AS IT IS A BOOK?

Tommy Wilhelm has lost his job, and now seems on the verge of losing his mind. Living temporarily in a hotel on Manhattan's upper Broadway, he is surrounded by a depressing gallery of old people, among them his coldly uncaring father. The city is too hot, the elevator doors are too slow, his money is running out, and the wife whom he left but who will not give him a divorce is pestering him for support payments. Worse, a shyster doctor has talked him into squandering his piddling savings on the commodities market. "What's the matter?" asks his father, to whom he turns as a last resort. "Everything," Tommy replies. "Just everything."

The PBS adaptation of Saul Bellow's 1956 novella Seize the Day stands apart from the usual run of prestige TV dramas... Despite widespread acclaim (and a Nobel prize for Literature in 1976), Saul Bellow has never before had a novel turned into a film.

It is hard to imagine anyone doing a better job. The adaptation, written by Ronald Ribman and directed by Fielder Cook, takes a few careful liberties with Bellow's story but packs its essence into a compact, ruefully funny and tensely moving 90 minutes. In odd but inspired casting, Robin Williams plays Tommy and delivers the best dramatic performance of his career. In past roles, Williams has sometimes seemed mechanical and pinched. Here his hyperactive face and vocal tics are orchestrated into a wrenching picture of panic and desperation.

Jerry Stiller, another actor known primarily for comedy, is equally impressive as the loud-mouthed charlatan Dr. Tamkin, who dispenses folk wisdom between gulps of pot roast and watermelon. Joseph Wiseman is a bit too pat as the unfeeling father, but there are some finely etched cameos from Katherine Borowitz, Tony Roberts, William Hickey, and particularly Jo Van Fleet as a dowager who defiantly stares down Tommy. (Bellow himself appears in a walk-through as a hotel guest.)

The modestly budgeted effort, from the producers responsible for a fine PBS adaptation of James Baldwin's Go Tell It on the Mountain, uses its resources well. The New York setting, for example, might have been sketched more elaborately. But a single scene of Tommy hustling an irascible old man (Tom Aldredge) across the street before the light changes conveys all that is needed. Trying to squeeze his car into a tight parking space, Tommy huffs mightily as he turns the steering wheel back and forth while his front-seat companion Dr. Tamkin rattles on: a perfect visual metaphor for Tommy's plight. The makers of Seize the Day did not settle for translating words to screen: somebody gave this one some thought.

From "Down and Out in Manhattan" by Richard Schickel. Copyright 1987 Time Inc. All rights reserved. Reprinted by permission from Time.

10. Which of the actors mentioned in the review was the author least impressed with?

(1) Robin Williams
(2) Jerry Stiller
(3) Joseph Wiseman
(4) Katherine Borowitz
(5) Tony Roberts

11. The author feels that Robin Williams' earlier dramatic performances were

(1) more convincing than his performance in Seize the Day
(2) not as convincing as his performance in Seize the Day
(3) humorous, though they were meant to be serious
(4) serious, though they were meant to be humorous
(5) just as satisfying as his role in Seize the Day

12. What is implied by the statement that the makers of this film "did not settle for translating words to screen" (lines 60-61)?

(1) This film could have been better.
(2) People who do film adaptations often rely solely on their source material and don't bother to be creative.
(3) The film lost something in the translation.
(4) The filmmakers will have to go to court for what they did to the book.
(5) The makers of this film went too far with their creativity.

13. Based on the review, what other situation might you expect to find in Seize the Day?

(1) Tommy spends a relaxing day in the park.
(2) Tommy gets stuck in a stalled subway car.
(3) Tommy enjoys a dinner and concert with a friend.
(4) Dr. Tamkin gives Tommy a good stock tip.
(5) Tommy is comforted by a talk with his father.

14. What function does the first paragraph of the review serve?

(1) It gives information that must be known to understand the film.
(2) It shows how the author was moved by the film.
(3) It praises the acting job of Robin Williams.
(4) It grabs the readers' interest.
(5) It explains why the author liked the film.

15. Why does the author include the information about Saul Bellow in paragraph two?

(1) to show off his own knowledge of literature
(2) to suggest the quality of the material the film was based on
(3) to draw a comparison between Bellow and other writers
(4) to criticize the choice of the adapters
(5) to explain the success of the adaptation

<u>Items 16 to 18</u> are based on the following poem.

WHAT DO THE SPEAKER'S GRANDMOTHERS MEAN TO HER?

Lineage

My grandmothers were strong.
They followed plows and bent to toil.
They moved through fields sowing seed.
They touched earth and grain grew.
They were full of sturdiness and singing.
My grandmothers were strong.

My grandmothers are full of memories
Smelling of soap and onions and wet clay
With veins rolling roughly over quick hands
They have many clean words to say.
My grandmothers were strong.
Why am I not as they?

"Lineage" by Margaret Walker. Copyright by the author. Reprinted by permission.

16. The details in the poem indicate that the speaker regards her grandmothers with

(1) suspicion
(2) awe
(3) indifference
(4) amusement
(5) embarrassment

17. What does the speaker wish for herself?

(1) that she could have happier memories of her grandmothers
(2) that she might never grow old
(3) that she might grow old as gracefully as her grandmothers have done
(4) that she could have her grandmothers' inner strength
(5) that she had been able to know her grandmothers better

18. Based on information in the passage, if the speaker were dealing with older people in a business setting, which of the following would she be most likely to recommend?

(1) shortened work hours
(2) increased medical benefits
(3) establishing an advisory council of older employees
(4) better retirement benefits
(5) mandatory retirement at age 60

Items 19 to 23 are based on the following passage.

DOES KARLIE WIN HIS FIGHT?

"Get off this seat!"

Karlie did not hear the gruff voice...

"Get up! I said, there are benches down there for you!"

Karlie stared up and said nothing. He stared up into very sharp, cold grey eyes.

"Can't you hear me speaking to you, you black swine!"

Slowly and deliberately Karlie puffed at his cigarette. So this was his test. They both stared at each other, challenged with the eyes, like two boxers, each knowing that they must eventually trade blows yet each afraid to strike first.

"Must I dirty my hands on scum like you?"

Karlie said nothing. To speak would be to break the spell, the supremacy he felt he was slowly gaining. An uneasy silence. Then,

"I will call a policeman rather than kick a Hotnot like you! You can't even open your black jaw when a white man speaks to you!"

Karlie saw the weakness. The white youth was afraid to take action himself. He, Karlie, had won the first round of the bench dispute!

A crowd now collected. "Afrika!" shouted one joker. Karlie ignored the remark. People were now milling around, staring at the unusual sight of a black man sitting on a white man's bench. Karlie merely puffed on....

"What is your name and address?"

Karlie still maintained his obstinate silence. It took the policeman rather unawares. The crowd was growing every minute.

"You have no right to speak to this man in such a manner!" It was the white lady in the blue dress.

"Mind your own business! I'll ask your help when I need it. It is people like you who make Kaffirs think they're as good as white people!"

Then addressing Karlie, "Get up, you!"

"I insist that you treat him with proper respect!"

The policeman turned red. "This...this...." He was at a loss for words.

"Kick up the Hotnot if he won't get up!" shouted a spectator. Rudely a white man laid hands on Karlie. "Get up you bloody bastard!"

Karlie turned to resist, to cling to the bench, his bench. There were more than one man now pulling at him. He hit out wildly and then felt a dull pain as somebody rammed a fist into his face. He was now bleeding and wild-eyed. He would fight for it. The constable clapped a pair of handcuffs round Karlie's wrists and tried to clear a way through the crowds. Karlie was still struggling. A blow or two landed on him. Suddenly he relaxed and slowly struggled to his feet. It was useless fighting any longer. Now it was his turn to smile. He had challenged and won. Who cared at the result?

From "The Bench" by Richard Rive. Copyright © 1958 by Drum Publications. Reprinted by permission of Faith Press, Ltd, London.

19. Karlie lives in a country where

(1) people enjoy violence and fighting
(2) policemen protect black people from racial prejudice
(3) black people and white people have equal rights
(4) there are no rules or laws
(5) white people have different rights from black people

20. What is the nature of Karlie's challenge?

(1) Karlie wants to show that he can sit anywhere he chooses.
(2) Karlie wants to lead the Kaffirs in a revolution.
(3) Karlie wants to prove that he deserves a good job.
(4) Karlie wants to show that he deserves a better education than he has received.
(5) Karlie wants to prove that all white people are stupid.

21. Why does Karlie stop resisting the arresting officer?

(1) He sees that the officer is much stronger than he is.
(2) He feels that he has won this fight.
(3) He does not want to make his situation worse by assaulting an officer.
(4) He is too weak to fight any longer.
(5) He realizes that no one in the crowd is on his side.

22. Why does the author include such details as the young man's "sharp, cold grey eyes," the lady's "blue dress," and Karlie's eventual "wild-eyed" expression?

(1) to make the sentences in the story longer
(2) to make the dialogue read at a quicker pace
(3) to create a contrast between the people's words and actions
(4) to show physical differences between white people and black people
(5) to help the readers imagine what the characters look like

23. The author creates an image of the white youth through

(1) dialogue only
(2) description only
(3) both dialogue and description
(4) Karlie's own words
(5) the policeman's words

Items 24 to 27 are based on the following passage.

HOW ARE ANTS AND PEOPLE SIMILAR?

One day when I went out to my wood-pile, or rather my pile of stumps, I observed two large ants, the one red, the other much larger, nearly half an inch long, and black, fiercely contending with one another. Having once got hold they never let go, but struggled and wrestled and rolled on the chips incessantly. Looking farther, I was surprised to find that the chips were covered with such combatants, that it was not a duellum but a bellum, a war between two races of ants, the red always pitted against the black, and frequently two red ones to one black. The legions of these Myrmidons covered all the hills and vales in my wood-yard, and the ground was already strewn with the dead and dying, both red and black. It was the only battle which I have ever witnessed, the only battle-field I ever trod while the battle was raging; internecine war; the red republicans on the one hand, and the black imperialists on the other. On every side they were engaged in deadly combat, yet without any noise that I could hear, and human soldiers never fought so resolutely. I watched a couple that were fast locked in each other's embraces, in a little sunny valley amid the chips, now at noonday prepared to fight till the sun went down, or life went out. The smaller red champion had fastened himself like a vice to his adversary's front, and through all the tumblings on that field never for an instant ceased to gnaw at one of his feelers near the root, having already caused the other to go by the board; while the stronger black one dashed him from side to side, and, as I saw on looking nearer, had already divested him of several of his members. They fought with more pertinacity than bulldogs. Neither manifested the least disposition to retreat. It was evident that their battle-cry was "Conquer or die."

"War of the Ants" by Henry David Thoreau

24. Where does the author witness this event?

(1) on a battlefield
(2) in a sunny valley
(3) by a pile of wood
(4) in a bed of flowers
(5) in the forest

25. The author was fascinated by the battle of the ants because

(1) he did not know there were ants in his yard
(2) he thought their fighting was humorous
(3) he had thought that the red and black ants got along peacefully
(4) he had never seen such a war close up before
(5) he was surprised that the smaller ants were winning the battle

26. The author implies in his description that the ants fight

(1) cautiously
(2) bravely
(3) savagely
(4) fearfully
(5) fairly

27. How does the author stress the similarity between the behavior of the ants and the behavior of people?

(1) by comparing the ants to bulldogs
(2) by using human terms to describe the ants
(3) by explaining the way the ants fight
(4) by revealing the ants' colors
(5) by describing his interest in the ants' actions

Items 28 to 31 are based on the following passage.

DOES ANNIE FACE AN IMPOSSIBLE TASK?

KATE: Is it possible, even? To teach a deaf-blind child half of what an ordinary child learns—has that ever been done?

ANNIE: Half?

KATE: A tenth.

ANNIE (reluctantly): No. (Kate's face loses its remaining hope, still appraising her youth.) Dr. Howe did wonders, but—an ordinary child? No, never. But then I thought when I was going over his reports—(She indicates the one in her hand.)—he never treated them like ordinary children. More like—eggs everyone was afraid would break.

KATE (A pause): May I ask how old you are?

ANNIE: Well, I'm not in my teens, you know! I'm twenty.

KATE: All of twenty.

ANNIE (Annie takes the bull by the horns, valiantly): Mrs. Keller, don't lose heart just because I'm not on my last legs. I have three big advantages over Dr. Howe that money couldn't buy for you. One is his work behind me, I've read every word he wrote about it and he wasn't exactly what you'd call a man of few words. Another is to be young, why, I've got energy to do anything. The third is, I've been blind. (But it costs her something to say this.)

KATE (Quietly): Advantages.

ANNIE (Wry): Well, some have the luck of the Irish, some do not.

KATE (Kate smiles; she likes her.): What will you try to teach her first?

ANNIE: First, last, and—in between, language.

KATE: Language.

ANNIE: Language is to the mind more than light is to the eye. Dr. Howe said that.

KATE: Language. (She shakes her head.) We can't get through to teach her to sit still. You are young, despite your years, to have such—confidence. Do you, inside?

ANNIE (Annie studies her face; she likes her, too.): No, to tell you the truth I'm as shaky inside as a baby's rattle!

KATE (They smile at each other, and Kate pats her hand.): Don't be.

From The Miracle Worker by William Gibson. Copyright © 1956, 1957 by the author. Reprinted by permission of Atheneum Publishing.

28. Why does Annie have a special understanding for blind children?
   (1) She is better trained than Dr. Howe.
   (2) She has a tremendous amount of confidence.
   (3) She went to an excellent school.
   (4) She was once blind herself.
   (5) She has worked with blind children for years.

29. What effect do Annie's answers have on Kate?
   (1) They make Kate doubt Annie's abilities.
   (2) They worry Kate.
   (3) They begin to convince Kate of Annie's worth.
   (4) They convince Kate that a deaf-blind child cannot be helped.
   (5) They assure Kate that miracles can happen.

30. Annie's comment "Language is to the mind more than light is to the eye" (lines 39–40) indicates her belief that
   (1) language is more important than light
   (2) language allows people to use their minds
   (3) it is better to speak than to see
   (4) it is possible to see without light
   (5) it is better to see than to use language

31. Why does the author give lines to his characters that are not complete sentences, such as Kate's "All of twenty" (line 18) and Annie's "First, last, and in between, language" (line 36–37).
   (1) to show that the characters are not well-educated
   (2) to create tension between the characters
   (3) to create a sense of warmth between the characters
   (4) so the actors will have shorter lines to remember
   (5) so the characters speak and sound like real people

Items 32 to 35 are based on the following passage.

WERE DINOSAURS STUPID ANIMALS?

Dinosaurs have been making a strong comeback of late, in this age of "I'm OK, you're OK." Most paleontologists are now willing to view them as energetic, active, and capable animals. The *Brontosaurus* that wallowed in its pond a generation ago is now running on land, while pairs of males have been seen twining their necks about each other in elaborate sexual combat for access to females (much like the neck wrestling of giraffes). Modern anatomical reconstructions indicate strength and agility, and many paleontologists now believe that dinosaurs were warmblooded.

The idea of warmblooded dinosaurs has captured the public imagination and received a torrent of press coverage. Yet another vindication of dinosaurian capability has received very little attention, although I regard it as equally significant. I refer to the issue of stupidity and its correlation with brain size. The revisionist interpretation, which I support in this column, does not enshrine dinosaurs as paragons of intellect, but it does maintain that they were not small brained after all. They had the "right-sized" brains for reptiles of their body size.

I don't wish to deny that the flattened, minuscule head of largebodied *Stegosaurus* houses little brain from our subjective, top-heavy perspective, but I do wish to assert that we should not expect more of the beast. First of all, large animals have relatively smaller brains than related, small animals. The correlation of brain size with body size among kindred animals (all reptiles, all mammals, for example) is remarkably regular. As we move from small to large animals, from mice to elephants or small lizards to Komodo dragons, brain size increases, but not so fast as body size. In other words, bodies grow fatter than brains, and large animals have low ratios of brain weight to body weight. In fact, brains only grow about two-thirds as fast as bodies. Since we have no reason to believe that large animals are consistently stupider than their smaller relatives, we must conclude that large animals require relatively less brain to do as well as smaller animals. If we do not recognize this relationship, we are likely to underestimate the mental power of very large animals, dinosaurs in particular.

From The Panda's Thumb by Stephen Jay Gould. Copyright © 1980 by the author. Reprinted by permission of W. W. Norton & Company.

32. The author is primarily concerned with
- **(1)** the mating habits of dinosaurs
- **(2)** the differences between dinosaurs and mammals
- **(3)** the superiority of warmblooded dinosaurs
- **(4)** the brain size of dinosaurs
- **(5)** the eating habits of dinosaurs

33. It can be concluded from the context that "paleontologists" (line 13) are
- **(1)** people who study dinosaurs
- **(2)** the skeletons of dinosaurs
- **(3)** a certain class of dinosaurs
- **(4)** the time period during which dinosaurs lived
- **(5)** prehistoric people

34. Based on the information in this passage, which of the following explanations of the extinction of dinosaurs would the author most likely reject?
- **(1)** They could not adjust to a change in climate.
- **(2)** They were caught in a meteor shower.
- **(3)** They could not compete when smarter animals appeared.
- **(4)** They were wiped out by an infectious disease.
- **(5)** They were victims of a terrible flood.

35. The author's main purpose in the passage is to
- **(1)** propose a course of action
- **(2)** argue an opinion
- **(3)** tell a story
- **(4)** provide information
- **(5)** offer a detailed description

Items 36 to 40 are based on the following poem.

WHAT HAPPENED IN BIRMINGHAM THAT DAY?

Ballad of Birmingham
(On the bombing of a church in Birmingham, Alabama, 1963)

"Mother dear, may I go downtown
Instead of out to play,
And march the streets of Birmingham
In a Freedom March today?"

"No, baby, no, you may not go,
For the dogs are fierce and wild,
And clubs and hoses, guns and jails
Aren't good for a little child."

"But, mother, I won't be alone.
Other children will go with me,
And march the streets of Birmingham
To make our country free."

"No, baby, no, you may not go,
For I fear those guns will fire.
But you may go to church instead
And sing in the children's choir."

She has combed and brushed her night-dark hair,
And bathed rose petal sweet,
And drawn white gloves on her small brown hands,
And white shoes on her feet.

The mother smiled to know her child
Was in the sacred place,
But that smile was the last smile
To come upon her face.

For when she heard the explosion,
Her eyes grew wet and wild.
She raced through the streets of Birmingham
Calling for her child.

She clawed through bits of glass and brick,
Then lifted out a shoe.
"O, here's the shoe my baby wore,
But, baby, where are you?"

NOTE: The poem is based on a historical incident. On September 15, 1963, a dynamite bomb exploded in a black church in Birmingham, killing four children.

"The Ballad of Birmingham," by Dudley Randall. Copyright © 1963 by the author. Reprinted by permission of Broadside Press.

36. What happens in the first four stanzas?

(1) a Freedom March is announced
(2) a conversation between mother and daughter
(3) a girl disobeys her mother
(4) a girl goes downtown
(5) a mother loses her daughter

37. Why doesn't the mother want the girl to go on the Freedom March?

(1) She is afraid the girl might get hurt.
(2) She doesn't want the girl to be with other children.
(3) She is not interested in making the country free.
(4) She is afraid the girl will miss singing in the choir.
(5) She doesn't want the child to dirty her white shoes.

38. What happens to the child because she went to the church?

(1) She loses her shoe.
(2) She angers her mother.
(3) She gets chased through the streets.
(4) She dies in an explosion.
(5) She joins the children's choir.

39. By using dialogue and telling about the incident in the form of a story, the poet

(1) softens the impact of the ending
(2) makes the ending more horrifying
(3) makes the incident seem less real
(4) tries to imitate a news report
(5) gets more quickly to the point

40. With which of the following would the poet most probably agree?

(1) Churches are always safe places.
(2) Children should stay away from Freedom Marches.
(3) Children should not always obey their parents.
(4) Tragedy can occur where we least expect it.
(5) Children should stay away from churches.

Items 41 to 45 are based on the following passage.

WHAT IS CLINTESSENCE?

In a Chicago video store last year, a teenager saw a cassette for The Rookie and said, "Look! The new Charlie Sheen movie!" That Sheen was billed below Clint Eastwood, who also directed the film, mattered not to this youth. Clint, long past his popular prime, was as old and irrelevant as Gary Cooper, Tom Mix, Methuselah. To many moviegoers, Eastwood, 62, has become the character he played in Sergio Leone's westerns 25 (and a million) years ago: the "Man with No Name."

All right then. If the young won't respect a living legend, a man has to tend to it himself. Unforgiven, Eastwood's first western since Pale Rider in 1985, is a dark, passionate drama with good guys so twisted and bad guys so persuasive that virtue and villainy become two views of the same soul. But it is also Eastwood's meditation on age, repute, courage, heroism—on all those burdens he has been carrying with such good grace for decades. On Clintessence.

Will Munny (Eastwood) is a gunfighter trying to escape the lure of notoriety. He's certainly lost the hang of it after years in retirement. He can't shoot straight or stay on a horse. And he is eager to dispel anyone's illusions of outlaw grandeur. In his prime he killed women and children; hell, he "killed just about everything that walks and crawls." And was he ever scared? "I can't remember. I was drunk most of the time."

Whatever he was—Will, Clint—he now sees his star in eclipse; "I ain't different from anybody else no more." So why is he riding into town with an old partner (Morgan Freeman) to go up against a tough sheriff (Gene Hackman) and collect the bounty on a couple of cowpokes who slashed a prostitute? He says it's for the money. But it's really because a man's job is his life. Will shoots people. Clint shoots westerns....

Frontier life was no idyll; it was filth and boredom punctuated by dumb gunplay. Manhood: why, that's just male vanity, and women can be mutilated for mocking it. The idea of straight shooting as an earnest of heroism—that's bunk too; it was mostly drunks killing drunks. Unforgiven even gets you musing about death in the movies....

All this might seem old-fashioned to a kid in a video store. But to anyone who appreciates what Clint Eastwood has meant to movies, old-fashioned is just another way of saying classic.

From Richard Corliss, "The Last Roundup," in Time, August 10, 1992, copyright Time, Inc. Reprinted by permission.

41. According to the reviewer, why do Will Munny and his partner ride into town?

(1) because they are drunk
(2) because they need money
(3) because they must do the job they have chosen as their life
(4) because they want to become famous
(5) because they are good guys

42. Which of the following best describes the character Clint Eastwood plays in this movie?

(1) the "Man with No Name"
(2) a cold-hearted killer
(3) a worn-out gunfighter
(4) a tough sheriff
(5) a confident hero

43. What does the reviewer suggest about the nature of Unforgiven?

(1) It is an ordinary western.
(2) It is more thoughtful than earlier shoot-em-up westerns.
(3) It has a lot of appeal for young audiences.
(4) It is based on Clint Eastwood's real-life experiences.
(5) It is too old-fashioned to succeed.

44. Why does the reviewer frame the article with the example of the kid in the video store?

(1) to explain why Clint Eastwood has been forgotten
(2) to emphasize the importance of appreciating a classic
(3) to introduce Clint Eastwood in his role as director
(4) to contrast Charlie Sheen and Clint Eastwood
(5) to suggest where Sergio Leone movies can be found

45. What function do the quotations from Will Munny serve in this review?

(1) They provide insight into how the character sees himself.
(2) They explain why the character went into retirement.
(3) They are examples of the drama in Unforgiven.
(4) They provide glimpses of frontier life.
(5) They help the reviewer introduce new ideas.

Answers are on pages 101–104.

Performance Analysis Chart

Directions: Circle the number of each item that you got correct on the Simulated Practice Test. Count how many items you got correct in each row; count how many items you got correct in each column. Write the amount correct per row and column as the numerator in the fraction in the appropriate "Total Correct" box. (The denominators represent the total number of items in the row or column.) Write the grand total correct over the denominator, **45**, at the lower right corner of the chart. (For example, if you got 40 items correct, write *40* so that the fraction reads 40/**45**.)

Item Type	Nonfiction (page 1)	Fiction (page 10)	Drama (page 19)	Poetry (page 28)	Commentary (page 38)	TOTAL CORRECT
Literal Comprehension	5, 6, 24, 32	1, 21	28	17, 36, 37	10,41,42	**/13**
Inferential Comprehension	7, 25, 26, 33	2, 19, 20	29, 30	16, 38	11, 12, 43	**/14**
Application	9, 34	3		18, 40	13	**/6**
Analysis	8, 27, 35	4, 22, 23	31	39	14, 15 44, 45	**/12**
TOTAL CORRECT	**/13**	**/9**	**/4**	**/8**	**/11**	**/45**

The page numbers in parentheses indicate where in this book you can find more exercises of the various types of literature and commentary and the types of questions you encountered on the Practice Test.

Answers and Explanations

Nonfiction Items

1. **(2)** *Literal Comprehension/Nonfiction.* In lines 1–28, the author focuses on a description of how Houdini mastered his art, eliminating (1). In lines 29–53, the author describes Houdini's virtues and relates a story that illustrates Houdini's integrity. Houdini may have been hard-working and pious, but he was also generous (which contradicts [3] and [4]).
2. **(3)** *Literal Comprehension/Nonfiction.* In lines 19–22, the author traces Houdini's talent to his days of working in a locksmith's shop.
3. **(3)** *Inferential Comprehension/Nonfiction.* In the first paragraph the author says that Houdini died as the result of "a blow by a college student, given under a misapprehension, when he was ill reading his mail." This detail—especially the term *misapprehension*—suggests that Houdini's death came about accidentally.
4. **(4)** *Analysis/Nonfiction.* By comparing Houdini with Lindbergh, someone else who was "fervent and unremitting" (lines 27–28), the author emphasizes that Houdini was completely devoted to becoming the best magician he could be.
5. **(1)** *Application/Nonfiction.* Houdini's devotion to his mother was "one of his most striking traits" (lines 40–42). It would be unlikely that he would forget her birthday. It is possible that his implied piety (lines 32–33) would lead him to a religious service (4), that his generosity (line 39) would make him charitable (2), and that his industrious nature (line 38) would inspire him to take two jobs (5). (3) is something he would have done out of loyalty and generosity.
6. **(5)** *Literal Comprehension/Nonfiction.* The author says that the reader "seemed to be a stranger" (line 3–4). He presumes that the man was a United States officer but is not certain.
7. **(4)** *Literal Comprehension/Nonfiction.* Rather than a feeling of bitterness, "there was pity among the slaves for our former owners" (lines 20–21). The slaves might have had good reason for some of the attitudes mentioned as choices; but according to the author, they felt sorry for their former owners.
8. **(3)** *Inferential Comprehension/Nonfiction.* Toward the end of the passage, the author discusses the problems that freedom poses for the older slaves. They are not strong enough to fend for themselves (lines 41–45), they do not know where to go (lines 45–46), and they have an emotional attachment to their owners (lines 48–52). All of these would discourage them from leaving. It is logical to assume that the "whispered conversations" concern some arrangement for staying on at the plantation.
9. **(1)** *Analysis/Nonfiction.* The author's use of the slaves' terms for their former masters underscores the "strange and peculiar attachment" (lines 48–50) many of the older slaves felt. The adjective "old" carries a sense of familiarity or affection. The phrases imply a link, not hatred (2), inhumanity (4), or betrayal (5).
10. **(4)** *Analysis/Nonfiction.* The author uses two methods to develop his discussion. He states a few facts about the situation, but he spends even more time analyzing those facts, making generalizations about the ways in which the slaves viewed them and giving his insights about their effects.
11. **(2)** *Literal Comprehension, Global/Nonfiction.* First with Dr. B, then at home with the rest of the family, the topic of conversation is how to help Karen. With the doctor the parents speak of her physical development, and with the family they speak of her emotional and social development; but in both cases the topic is helping Karen to grow up with a sense of self-worth.
12. **(3)** *Analysis/Nonfiction.* The most emotional point of the passage—the point that appeals most to the reader's own emotions—is Jimmy's reaction to Dr. B's bleak news (lines 16–22). None of the techniques described in the other choices are used in this passage.
13. **(2)** *Inferential Comprehension/Nonfiction.* (4) and (5) are not hinted at in the passage. Although Jimmy is upset (3), there is nothing to suggest that he will remain so once a solution has been found. Although Dr. B paints a grim picture for disabled children (1), he shows Karen's parents that such a future need not be

true for Karen, especially with their help. Both from the parents' conversation with Dr. B and from the discussion at home, it seems that family members are making decisions that will affect their futures dramatically.

14. **(1)** *Inferential Comprehension/Nonfiction.* Dr. B is very practical; he states the facts about the probable futures of most children with cerebral palsy rather unemotionally. However, he subsequently makes it clear to the parents that they can give Karen a better future than that. That he is intense can be inferred from his habit of chain-smoking (lines 9–11).

15. **(4)** *Application/Nonfiction.* One of the family's new rules is this: "Many folk with agile limbs are handicapped in the true sense, by a phony set of values, faulty character, etc." (lines 44–46). The family does not see physical or mental disabilities—which cannot be helped—as nearly as bad a handicap as character flaws—which, presumably, can be helped.

16. **(1)** *Analysis/Nonfiction.* In a true account of a serious problem, the names of well-known people are often altered. None of the other choices would explain the use of only an initial.

17. **(3)** *Literal Comprehension/Nonfiction.* Although all of the choices are stated or implied at some point in the passage, the only purpose that is stated again and again is that the author is refusing to accept the Pulitzer Prize and that he has good reasons for doing so.

18. **(4)** *Analysis/Nonfiction.* In the section in which he mentions blasphemy, the author also refers to those who award literary prizes as "a college of cardinals" (line 35). These references imply that the committee believes itself to have power similar to that of a religious body. The warning is against the committee's growing belief that it alone has the right and wisdom to judge good writing.

19. **(4)** *Analysis/Nonfiction.* The author follows his quote by explaining that it means that there is no set standard for judgment. Rather, judgment would seem to be made only "in obedience to whatever code of Good Form may chance to be popular at the moment" (lines 25–27).

20. **(2)** *Analysis/Nonfiction.* Although the author does not agree with the ideas of the Pulitzer Prize Committee, he expresses his disagreement in polite terms. Note particularly the greeting and closing of the letter, in which the author takes special care to address the committee politely.

21. **(1)** *Application/Nonfiction.* In his letter, Sinclair Lewis warns other writers that they are compromising themselves by accepting prizes (lines 45–52). He states, "Only by regularly refusing the Pulitzer Prize can novelists keep [a censoring] power from being permanently set up over them" (lines 41–44). Since he sees the rejection of awards as the way to keep books "free," he probably would offer the same suggestion for keeping movies "free."

22. **(2)** *Literal Comprehension/Nonfiction.* In the first sentence, the author says, "I have always been annoyed with the inequality of alterations" (lines 3–5). The other choices do come in for humorous criticism at points, but the story that the author uses to illustrate her point is a continual contrast that tells how "inequal" the alterations are.

23. **(3)** *Inferential Comprehension/Nonfiction.* Since the rest of the passage deals with the author's experiences in clothing stores, it can be assumed that the mention of the needle is a reference to her inability to sew well.

24. **(2)** *Analysis/Nonfiction.* The comparison is unusual and funny. Along with other odd images, it adds humor to the author's discussion. It is not meant to be a literal description.

25. **(5)** *Literal Comprehension/Nonfiction.* Each of the author's requests for an alteration is responded to by a statement of how much the alteration would cost.

26. **(2)** *Application/Nonfiction.* The whole point of the article is that men are given better treatment than women are. Although this instance is limited to clothing alterations, the author would probably think that any discrimination is unfair.

27. **(3)** *Literal Comprehension/Nonfiction.* The first sentence states that the town has about ninety people. The rest of the description supports the image of a small town.

28. **(2)** *Literal Comprehension/Nonfiction.* The man who answers the door and later the author's questions is identified as Thurmond Watts. Senator Gore is present only in a poster.

29. **(2)** *Inferential Comprehension/Nonfiction.* In line 25, the author asks "If this is Nameless..." but does not mention a map (1), a reading problem (3), or being lost (4). The only possible explanation given in the passage comes when Watts explains why there aren't any identifying road signs (lines 60–63).

30. **(4)** *Inferential Comprehension/Nonfiction.* The story about the town's name (lines 47–54) add up to this conclusion. None of the suggestions were accepted until the last fellow made his annoyed remark. None of the other choices are supported.

31. **(1)** *Inferential Comprehension/Nonfiction.* Miss Ginnie says that her husband knows the story as well as she. As the story is told, they both add details and correct details, showing a long familiarity with the story. This process contradicts the other choices.

32. **(2)** *Application/Nonfiction.* Judging by the way Nameless was named, the odd names of the other towns probably have interesting histories. There is no other likely reason suggested about the towns.

Fiction Items

1. **(2)** *Inferential Comprehension/Fiction.* The passage opens with Mr. White's expression of a wish to see India for himself thus eliminating Choice (1). Apparently something about India has just been discussed. Although the topic could have been temples (3), it seems more likely from the discussion that follows that the topic of the conversation had been more general and more closely related to Morris himself.

2. **(4)** *Literal Comprehension, Specific/Fiction.* The sergeant-major's initial reaction is to dismiss the subject quickly. He says that the story is "nothing worth hearing" (line 14). When pressed for details, he tries to discuss the subject casually. It is only when the family draws the information out of him that he opens up and prepares to tell the full story.

3. **(2)** *Literal Comprehension/Fiction.* This characteristic is stated in lines 40–42. (1) and (3) may be true but they don't make the monkey's paw special.

4. **(3)** *Inferential Comprehension/Fiction.* The sergeant-major's fear of the monkey's paw can be inferred from several details. He is reluctant to talk about it at all, trying first to change the subject and then introducing it only gradually. When Herbert questions his involvement in the story, Morris turns pale (line 51). The way in which he finally begins to tell the story erases all trace of humor from the group (lines 62–63).

5. **(4)** *Literal Comprehension/Fiction.* The last sentence of the passage states that "a hush fell upon the group." The reactions mentioned in (1), (2) and (3) occurred earlier in the passage.

6. **(2)** *Analysis/Fiction.* The slowness with which details are revealed helps to create a suspenseful atmosphere. So do the sergeant-major's fear, the news that the first man who used the monkey's paw wished for death (lines 59–61), and the family's reaction to this news.

7. **(3)** *Inferential Comprehension/Fiction.* In lines 38–40, Mrs. Jones gives the boy ten dollars with which to buy blue suede shoes. She warns him against snatching pocketbooks "because shoes come by devilish like that will burn your feet" (lines 42–43). Apparently snatching her pocketbook was the "devilish" way he had planned to "come by" the shoes.

8. **(3)** *Analysis/Fiction.* Just before the statement is made, the boy wonders what will happen to him next. He notices the open door and realizes that he "could make a dash for it" (line 17). He is giving serious consideration to leaving, and the repetition of *run* emphasizes his thought.

9. **(4)** *Literal Comprehension/Fiction.* Mrs. Jones fixes them both something to eat (lines 33–34); then she gives him ten dollars with which to buy blue suede shoes (lines 38–40).

10. **(2)** *Inferential Comprehension/Fiction.* At the opening of the passage, Mrs. Jones's words to the boy seem very angry (5). However, she soon admits to some kinship with the boy in that both of them have wanted things that they could not get (lines 21–22). She even admits to him that she is ashamed of some of the things she has done to get those things (lines 31–33). Her sympathy is demonstrated most strongly when she gives him food and money and then sends him on his way with only a warning.

11. **(3)** *Analysis/Fiction.* The pause is preceded by the woman saying "I wasn't going to say that" (line 30) and followed by further explanation. It is clear that the woman wants to be careful about what she does say to the boy so she stops to think. The emotions mentioned in the other choices are not suggested in the passage.

12. **(1)** *Application/Fiction.* Mrs. Jones ends their conversation with a warning not to steal and then sends him off with a "Behave yourself, boy!" (lines 48–49). The boy never sees her again, thus eliminating (4). (3) and (5) are too extreme to be supported by the passage. The boy's family is never discussed, thus eliminating (2). What the boy has learned from Mrs. Jones is that victims of crime are people, with their own personalities, disappointments, and dreams. He probably will remember that lesson if he thinks of stealing again—and, as a result, he may not steal.

13. **(5)** *Literal Comprehension/Fiction.* Ricardo concludes his argument with the photographer by declaring, "We are people and must be given attention as people" (lines 38–39).

14. **(1)** *Inferential Comprehension, Global/Fiction.* Ricardo becomes very angry when the photographer tries to use his home and son for "local color." He repeatedly makes the point that he does not like being treated like a cardboard cutout. This evidence suggests that Ricardo is a proud man—not in the sense that he is egotistical, but that he has a strong sense of self-worth.

15. **(1)** *Analysis/Fiction.* The author wants to emphasize the contrast between the way the photographer has treated Ricardo's son and the way the boy should be treated. The contrast is that between an object and a human being. The cutouts are lifeless imitations of human beings. The other choices do not reflect this contrast.

16. **(2)** *Application/Fiction.* Since Ricardo is a proud man with a strong sense of the "humanity" of people, he probably could not be "bribed" into compromising his views. He recognizes his poverty and his needs (lines 27–30), but he seems to care more about human understanding than he does about the elegance of his surroundings.

17. **(2)** *Literal Comprehension/Fiction.* The grandmother mentions the escaped criminal (1) in lines 13–15 and her preference for east Tennessee (3) in lines 34–35. She refers to the children's previous visit to Florida (4) in lines 29–30, following that statement with advice that the parents broaden the children's horizons (5) in lines 31–34.

18. **(4)** *Literal Comprehension/Fiction.* A baby is mentioned in line 29. Two older children—John Wesley and June Star—are mentioned in lines 37 and 41.

19. **(5)** *Inferential Comprehension/Fiction.* The children talk back to their grandmother and offer unflattering comments about her to the rest of the family. They show a distinct lack of manners and a lack of care for their grandmother. Of the choices given, "undisciplined" (5) best fits their behavior.

20. **(3)** *Inferential Comprehension/Fiction.* Two examples of the ways in which the members of the family disregard the grandmother are that Bailey and his wife ignore her when she talks to them and that the children do not stop what they are doing when they speak to her.

21. **(1)** *Analysis/Fiction.* In this comparison, the author states that the mother's face is "as broad and as innocent as a cabbage." It is not a physical trait that she is describing; rather, it is her way of commenting on the woman's bland character.

22. **(2)** *Literal Comprehension/Fiction.* The passage opens with the father's complaint, "I got nothing for you" and Maybelle's response, "Everybody out of work now" (line 5). The focus of the remainder of the passage is on the father's attempt to cope with his continued joblessness.

23. **(3)** *Inferential Comprehension/Fiction.* Since Maybelle mentions that "Mrs. Ellis is real nice about giving me things" in the same sentence in which she says, "I git paid every week," it can be inferred that Maybelle works for Mrs. Ellis in some capacity.

24. **(3)** *Application/Fiction.* The description of the father in lines 36–40 indicates that he is a loving man who cares deeply for his family. It would be out of character for him to beat the children (5) or Maybelle (4). He cherishes his ability to provide for his family, not wanting "white folks' leavings" (lines 24–25), which eliminates (1) and (2). The speaker mentions that the father has whittled toys for the children (lines 36–37); making a kite would be in keeping with that kind of behavior.

25. **(1)** *Analysis/Fiction.* When everything is "out of tune," it is uncertain, not following the expected pattern. The comparison calls attention to the fact that things are not going as expected for the family, as well as to the speaker's confusion.

26. **(4)** *Literal Comprehension/Fiction.* The speaker's question "Where did I fit into this crazy picture?" (line 51–52) immediately follows her conclusion that her mother was now the strength of the

family whereas her father now seemed as helpless as a tiny child. The parents' roles have altered drastically, and the speaker does not know how to make sense of the change.

27. **(4)** *Inferential Comprehension/Fiction.* A poor rural area is suggested by the buzzards sitting on the roof of the house next door in the opening lines of the passage. The "crumbling ceiling and a dusty spider web with spider's eggs and dead insects" (lines 112–114) also suggest this setting. There are no details to suggest a setting in a city (1), in the mountains (2), on an island (3) or on a river (5).

28. **(3)** *Inferential Comprehension/Fiction.* When the dentist tells the mayor he will take out his tooth without using any painkiller, we are told: "The Mayor looked him in the eye. 'All right,' he said, and tried to smile." (lines 75–76) The dentist makes all his preparations "without looking at the Mayor. But the Mayor didn't take his eyes off him." (lines 84–86) These details all suggest that the mayor, who is at the mercy of a man who hates him, regards the dentist with suspicion. These details support none of the other choices.

29. **(5)** *Analysis/Fiction.* This question might be answered best by eliminating the choices that are not believable on the basis of the characters and the situation. (1) can be eliminated because it is unlikely that there would be twenty dentists in a poor rural area or that the mayor would kill them all. It may be believable that a dictator like the mayor would kill twenty children of one man, but then the dentist probably would refer to them as "my children," not "our men"; so eliminate (3). Though the reference to "our men" suggests that the dentist may be the leader of a group opposed to the mayor, nothing suggests the two men are from different countries, so eliminate (2). (However, if he were the leader of the group he probably would call them "my men.") The dentist's statement cannot be interpreted very believably to mean what choice (4) states. (5) is therefore the most likely conclusion you can draw about the meaning of his statement.

30. **(4)** *Application/Fiction.* The main action of the passage shows that although the dentist hates the mayor, and blames him for violence committed against him, he gives the mayor medical (dental) care to relieve his suffering. In lines 40–41, he seems to consider using a gun against the mayor, but as soon as he sees the man's swollen face, he takes pity on him. The dentist is not completely against violence, however, since he tortures the mayor by refusing to use anesthesia. He also refers to a violent conflict between "our men" and the mayor's side, in which the mayor killed twenty of the dentist's political comrades (See question 29). Therefore, (5) is incorrect. Since he blames the mayor for this violent action and tortures him for it, (3) is also not correct. Although he at first pretends not to be home when the mayor arrives, he does not run away, so (1) and (2) are also wrong.

31. **(3)** *Inferential Comprehension/Fiction.* For the mayor to say that "the town" (the town government) and himself are "the same damn thing" plainly implies that he completely controls the town government. Nothing supports the interpretations in the other choices.

32. **(1)** *Analysis/Fiction.* You may arrive at the correct answer most efficiently by first eliminating the wrong choices. (2) and (3) can be eliminated because the mayor does not become sympathetic as a character when he is suffering (2) and shows no signs of being reformed by kindness (3). The end of the passage contradicts (4). Since the mayor is a dictator, (5) is not likely to be the theme of the excerpt. As for (1) — the correct answer — if you feel that the dentist is unkind to the mayor because he does not use any painkiller, you must still recognize that the dentist's kindly instincts keep him from taking advantage of the situation to injure the mayor or remove him from power. Moreover, the reason he gives for not using painkiller ("Because you have an abscess") may be truthful. He also shows his kindly instincts when he agrees to pull the mayor's tooth although he hates him, when he gives him a cloth to dry his tears, and when he tells him to "Go to bed... and gargle with salt water." The result of his kindness is that the mayor-dictator remains in power and treats him with open contempt at the end of the story.

Drama Items

1. **(4)** *Literal Comprehension/Drama.* In his first statement, Chris mentions "a hundred and twenty cracked engine-heads" (lines 3–4).
2. **(2)** *Inferential Comprehension/Drama.* Among the statements that identify the equipment as belonging to airplanes are Keller's defense "I thought they'd stop 'em before anybody took off" (lines 27–28) and Chris's statements "You even knew they wouldn't hold up in the air" (lines 48–49) and "Kids were hanging in the air by those heads" (lines 60–61).
3. **(2)** *Inferential Comprehension/Drama.* Keller summarizes the argument he has made throughout the passage by saying, "Chris... Chris, I did it for you, it was a chance and I took it for you. I'm sixty-one years old, when would I have another chance to make something for you?" (lines 42–46). He concludes by saying, "For you, a business for you!" (line 62).
4. **(5)** *Application/Drama.* Since Chris is horrified that his father sold defective equipment to save his business, he probably feels that, among the choices given, maintaining your integrity is the most important thing.
5. **(3)** *Analysis/Drama.* Keller appeals to his son for understanding and tries to make excuses for himself. His pleading tone helps to arouse the pity of the audience. The only other tone that appears to any extent in this passage is that of anger (1) but that is Chris's anger, not Keller's.
6. **(1)** *Inferential Comprehension/Drama.* The props described in the stage directions—for example, a sofa (line 19) and drapes (line 35) indicate that the scene occurs within the couple's house.
7. **(2)** *Literal Comprehension/Drama.* Phyllis defines Arthur's profession when she reminds him, "Your business is in this town" (lines 40–41).
8. **(2)** *Inferential Comprehension/Drama.* Phyllis worries that the neighbors will think them odd for wanting "to let an ex-convict live with us" (lines 28–29). Her concern, which is the basis of the argument in this passage, suggests that the neighbors oppose the idea of an ex-convict living in their community.
9. **(4)** *Analysis/Drama.* Many of the stage directions reveal Arthur's reactions to Phyllis's argument. In particular, when she has him look out the window, the stage directions say, "(*...it begins to sink in*)" (lines 36–37). After the stage direction (*...not knowing what to say next*)" (lines 49–50), Phyllis makes the point that ends the argument—in her favor.
10. **(3)** *Application/Drama.* Phyllis declares herself to be "crazy with fear because I don't want to be different" (lines 19–20). She probably would not take the chance of buying an experimental painting, which almost certainly would be "different." All of the other choices involve doing things that are popular or otherwise acceptable.
11. **(2)** *Analysis/Drama.* The dashes separate parts of the actors' speeches. They take the place of a stage direction indicating a pause. The other choices would not work well in the context of the speeches.
12. **(4)** *Literal Comprehension/Drama.* In her first speech, Jennie says to George, "I have literally just walked in the door" (lines 3–4).
13. **(3)** *Inferential Comprehension/Drama.* George wants to get the "date" over with, and he is insistent that Jennie agree with him. He gets to the point quickly, yet with some humor. In the lines specified, George gives two clues that also support this idea. First, he is "a very busy man" (line 25), and second, he likes "quiet" and "few distractions" (lines 25–26).
14. **(3)** *Literal Comprehension/Drama.* George's wish to meet Jennie is the reason for his telephone call; it is discussed throughout the passage. He states that the meeting would be "in the interest of moving on with our lives" (lines 27–28). He also states that it would allow Leo and Faye to feel "that they have fulfilled their noble mission in life" (lines 40–41)—a mission that he has previously defined as making them "have that inevitable date" (lines 19–20).
15. **(2)** *Inferential Comprehension/Drama.* Early in the passage, Jessie tells Mama, "You have no earthly idea how I feel" (line 8). As the passage continues, it becomes apparent that Jessie and Mama differ strongly in the way they think about Jessie's fantasies, her seizures, and Cecil's leaving. In each case, Mama reveals that she knows more about the subject than Jessie has told her.

16. **(1)** *Inferential Comprehension, Specific/Drama.* In trying to define what she means as "over there," Mama says, "Do people [over there] always say the right thing or get whatever they want, or what?" (lines 13–15). These are characteristics of a fantasy, not the real world; and Jessie never denies that she believes in her fantasies.

17. **(5)** *Literal Comprehension/Drama.* Jessie sees cigarettes as a source of stability in her unstable world. As she tells Mama, "Smoking is the only thing I know that's always just what you think it's going to be. Just like it was the last time and right there when you want it and real quiet" (lines 35–39).

18. **(4)** *Analysis/Drama.* The rapid succession of questions creates a sense of tension. It suggests that Mama is feeling frustrated by Jessie's refusal to share information about her life.

19. **(4)** *Application/Drama.* Mama has not yet been satisfied with Jessie's responses. She probably will continue to press Jessie for straight answers. Mama shows no evidence of accepting Jessie as she is (1), nor does Jessie show more of an inclination to admit to her fantasies (3).

20. **(1)** *Literal Comprehension/Drama.* Early in the passage, Liza asks, "I've won your bet for you, haven't I?" (lines 15–16). Higgins responds with the exclamation, "You won my bet! You!" (line 18).

21. **(5)** *Inferential Comprehension/Drama.* In addition to Higgins's insensitive comments to Liza throughout the passage (the strongest, perhaps, being "How the devil do I know what's become of you? What does it matter what becomes of you?" [lines 43–45]), Liza calls him a "selfish brute" (lines 23–24) and declares, "You wouldn't care if I was dead" (line 47).

22. **(4)** *Literal Comprehension/Drama.* The phrase "in the gutter" implies Liza's poverty. It is not likely, therefore, that they would have met in a store (2) or at a party (5). Neither a roadside stand (1) nor a carriage (3) are mentioned.

23. **(4)** *Application/Drama.* Throughout the passage, Higgins shows a high disregard for women—at least, for Liza. Even though she has made money for him by allowing him to win a bet, he claims that it was not her doing (lines 18–19). He refuses to listen to her; rather, he seems to find her silly, overemotional, and unworthy of his notice. If he feels about all women as he does about Liza—and nothing in the passage indicates that he singles out Liza for special consideration—then he probably would find "equal pay for equal work" a ridiculous notion.

24. **(3)** *Analysis/Drama.* Higgins refers to Liza as "presumptuous insect" (line 19), "creature" (line 31), and "you cat" (line 36). By refusing to allow Higgins to admit Liza's humanity, the playwright encourages the support of all but the most insensitive audience to stand behind Liza rather than Higgins.

25. **(2)** *Literal Comprehension/Drama.* Dr. Emerson identifies the setting as that of a hospital when he explains to Ken "This unit is for critical patients" and expresses his hope that Ken soon will be moved to a "much more comfortable, quiet hospital" (lines 11–15).

26. **(1)** *Inferential Comprehension/Drama.* Ken's realism can be seen in that he presses Dr. Emerson to be honest about his prognosis. Nevertheless, there is a twinge of bitterness, too, as evidenced in Ken's challenging "Really?" (line 6) and his comment about "vegetables" and "the vegetable store" (lines 16–17).

27. **(3)** *Inferential Comprehension/Drama.* The context of Ken's remark is the possibility of his condition's stabilizing and his being moved to a quieter facility despite his poor prognosis. Ken is referring to people who need care—in particular, people whose disabilities are so great that they are about as active as vegetables.

28. **(3)** *Inferential Comprehension/Drama.* Ken asks the doctor if he will be able to walk or use his arms. It can be concluded from these questions that at present he can use neither his arms nor legs. Although (1) or (2) might have caused the problem, neither is suggested in the passage.

29. **(4)** *Literal Comprehension, Global/Drama.* The topic of the contents of the window-seat is introduced in line 12 and continues for the rest of the passage. All of the other questions receive some treatment in the passage; only the question in (4), however, serves as an overall topic.

30. **(3)** *Literal Comprehension, Global/Drama.* The identity of the murderers—a subject that drives the conversation—is revealed when Martha states that she and Abby put poison in Adam Hoskins's wine (lines 46–48).

31. **(1)** *Inferential Comprehension, Specific/Drama.* Mortimer says that Teddy must go to Happy Dale because he is no longer "harmless" and therefore "has to be confined" (lines 1–3). These details suggest that "Happy Dale" is some kind of institution for the mentally ill.

32. **(4)** *Analysis/Drama.* The actions established by the playwright indicate that Abby and Martha act as though nothing unusual has happened. The playwright uses this action to indicate that they are not disturbed by Mortimer's news; rather, they have known about it all along.

Poetry Items

1. **(2)** *Inferential Comprehension/Poetry.* The combination of fountains, birds, and grass makes it very likely that the place is a park.

2. **(5)** *Inferential Comprehension/Poetry.* Lines 8–9 speak of the birds as being "Sure in these/pleasures there could not be a pain to bear." In other words, the happiness of the birds makes the poet even sadder, and so the birds are thoughtless because they do not consider the poet's pain.

3. **(1)** *Application/Poetry.* The entire poem examines the fact that the poet's pain is increased because nothing has changed in the park. It says specifically that "It was because the place was just the same/that made your absence seem a savage force" (lines 11–12). It is reasonable to assume, therefore, that if the place were changed, it would be less likely to remind her of her lost loved one so that her pain might be lessened.

4. **(4)** *Analysis/Poetry.* The poet compares her thoughts and feelings to an earthquake that could shake the earth (lines 14–15). This is very effective in conveying the strength of her emotions. (3) is incorrect because the poet does not show anger, only sadness. (5) is incorrect because the poet shows nature as cheerful; if she portrayed nature as a reflection of her emotions, it would be sad. There is no evidence for the other choices.

5. **(1)** *Literal Comprehension/Poetry.* Line 1 states that the two people had "last met" in this place. The speaker does not state how they had felt (2) and (3) there or how she feels about what happened there (5).

6. **(1)** *Literal Comprehension, Global/Poetry.* The speaker states that his vision "Left its seeds while I was sleeping" (line 4). The vision itself, which is described in the rest of the song, begins with the speaker's "In restless dreams I walked alone" (line 7).

7. **(2)** *Inferential Comprehension/Poetry.* In the third stanza there is the mention of "People talking without speaking" (line 15) and "People hearing without listening" (line 16). It is later stated that "no one dares disturb the sound of silence" (line 18) and "Silence like a cancer grows" (line 20). This evidence suggests that the main concern in the song focuses on the breakdown of personal communication.

8. **(5)** *Application/Poetry.* The most striking details in the third stanza are those that deal with a failure to communicate (lines 15–17). Of the choices given, (2), (3), and (4) deal with people by themselves, not in communication with others. (1) might be interpreted as a kind of communication, but "watching without seeing" (5) is a much clearer kind of failed communication.

9. **(3)** *Analysis/Poetry.* In context, the image is of something that is separated from the mass of humanity. People who love flash and color are worshipping a "neon God" (line 26), but this God's message can be found, not where these people are, but on graffiti-covered "subway walls and tenement halls." It is not a happy image, thus eliminating (2), (4), and (5), but neither does it imply a sense of reverence (1). Rather, it stresses the isolation that the speaker discusses throughout the song.

10. **(1)** *Analysis/Poetry.* By repeating "the sound of silence" or a variant of the phrase at the end of each stanza, the poet underscores the lack of communication he sees in society. The other choices are supporting and descriptive details.

11. **(2)** *Literal Comprehension, Specific/Poetry.* The speaker says that he heard the girl's voice "over the wires" (line 2)—a good description of a telephone conversation.

12. **(2)** *Inferential Comprehension/Poetry.* It can be assumed from statements such as "i felt suddenly/dizzy/With the jostling and shouting of merry flowers" (lines 3–5) and "I was whirled and tossed into delicious dancing" (line 12) that the speaker is overjoyed to hear from his "dear girl" (line 18).

13. **(3)** *Analysis/Poetry.* By using the word "up" alone on two consecutive lines, the poet adds a strong impression of a very small word. He creates a visual image of

upward movement that reflects the speaker's soaring spirits.

14. **(5)** *Inferential Comprehension/Poetry.* A separation of some length and perhaps distance is suggested by the fact that the woman's voice came "over time/and tide" (lines 20 and 21). This inference is also supported by the delighted reaction of the speaker. There is no support for (1), (2) or (3). The speaker and his girlfriend may live together (4), but their living arrangements are not even hinted at.
15. **(4)** *Literal Comprehension/Poetry.* The key to identity of the speakers is "We/left school" (lines 1–2). The speakers are not students at any school thus eliminating (1) and (3). The references to gin in line 6 (2) and jazz in line 7 (5) do not identify the speakers as clearly as does "We/left school."
16. **(3)** *Inferential Comprehension/Poetry.* Details throughout the poem, especially in the last sentence, show that the pool players' lifestyle is destructive—self-destructive. The poet's pool players appear aimless (lines 1–3) and pleasure seeking (lines 4–7); they die young (lines 7–8). Their lives would not normally be described by the words in (1), (2), (4), or (5).
17. **(2)** *Analysis/Poetry.* The poet uses simple sentence structure, informal language, and even slang to capture the way the speakers would actually talk, as in the examples "We real cool" (line 1) and "We/Sing sin" (lines 4–5). The language is "poetic" (3) only in that it appears in poetic form; otherwise, it is quite unlike language that usually is considered "poetic."
18. **(2)** *Analysis/Poetry.* The lines are short and rhythmical, sounding almost like a verbal strut. They echo the syncopation of jazz. The snappiness of the lines is not at all slow (1), soft (3) or drawn out (5). A military march would be more rigid or forceful (4).
19. **(2)** *Inferential Comprehension/Poetry.* Earlier the speaker has stated that night is falling, darkness is coming. In lines 9 and 10, the speaker suggests that the sense of loneliness will increase and so will the cover of darkness that will contribute to the snow's lack of expression. None of the other choices suggest the description of blackness.
20. **(4)** *Literal Comprehension/Poetry.* In lines 1–4 the speaker describes a snow-covered field that he is passing. It is that field, more so than any of the details that the speaker mentions in the first stanza, that is the most likely reference for "it" in line 5.
21. **(5)** *Inferential Comprehension/Poetry.* The speaker calls himself "absent-spirited" (line 7) and refers to his loneliness several times in the poem. These details, together with the bleak images the poet uses, suggest that the speaker is feeling lonely.
22. **(4)** *Analysis/Poetry.* A desert is an open, empty place, thus eliminating (2). In the final stanza, in particular, the speaker talks about the empty spaces inside himself and refers to them as his own "desert places." The choice of the expression helps to symbolize the speaker's feeling of emptiness. There is no evidence in the poem for (1); the speaker does not dwell on the details suggested by (3) or (5).
23. **(1)** *Literal Comprehension/Poetry.* The man was imprisoned because "he stole a box of crackers" (line 15) and because, in trying to get away, "he killed his pursuer" (line 19).
24. **(3)** *Inferential Comprehension/Poetry.* The expression is preceded by "tear-soaked bread" (line 11), indicating sadness. It is followed by his memory of what has caused his imprisonment. As that memory is described in lines 14–20, it seems that the sick, hungry daughter is the focus, and that the prisoner grieves because he will never see his daughter again.
25. **(5)** *Analysis/Poetry.* There is no evidence in the poem for any of the choices except (5). It is sadly ironic that the prisoner, though jailed, has his need for food supplied whereas his daughter, for whom he committed the crime that put him in prison, has starved to death (lines 23–24).
26. **(2)** *Analysis/Poetry.* There is no sense of happiness in this poem, thus eliminating (1) and (3), nor is there a sense of awe or worship (4). The prisoner seems too involved in his grief to feel any frustration toward his captors (5). Instead, he is a prisoner not only of his captors but of time itself (lines 3–4), and his thoughts seem to focus only on sad memories.
27. **(1)** *Inferential Comprehension/Poetry.* The speaker explains her command in the next line: "I'm fading away" (line 2). Later in the poem she states that she has become "more difficult/to hold" (lines 14–15). Although she does not speak

with shame (line 3) or desperation (line 2), she is lonely, and she seems not to expect the situation to improve.

28. **(5)** *Literal Comprehension/Poetry.* The speaker mentions "the gray of my mornings" and "the blues of every night" (lines 3–4).

29. **(2)** *Analysis/Poetry.* The "popping" reference is made before social workers (3) or psychologists (4) are mentioned. The only thing that the speaker says concerning the other people's view of her (5) is that she is "not an easy woman/to want" (lines 16–17). Overall, the speaker gives the impression of someone who is giving in rather than fighting, thus eliminating (1). Along with the other details in this stanza, the speaker gives the impression of things going wrong and not being able to put them right.

30. **(2)** *Analysis/Poetry.* The line is twice the length of all the others. The length calls attention to the three types of experts named. All deal with social situations, and none seem to have a solution for the problem of the decade.

Commentary Items

1. **(2)** *Literal Comprehension/Commentary.* Country music is mentioned several times as the music of the show.

2. **(5)** *Literal Comprehension/Commentary.* The variety of dancers is described in paragraph four. The skill level ranges from beginner to expert.

3. **(4)** *Inferential Comprehension/Commentary.* Throughout the review, the author describes people having fun. In the last sentence, the author refers more specifically to his own reaction. The show gives him "relief" because he can "smile to" it. He clearly enjoys the show. He also suggests the broad appeal (2) of the show by saying that country music has rid itself of an old image (line 2) and the generation gap (lines 47–49).

4. **(1)** *Analysis/Commentary.* The discussion of dances directly follows the statement that this is a "show about having fun" (line 25). The author's intention is to give an example of what kind of fun the people are having. (2), (3), and (4) refer to other shows, not Club Dance.

5. **(1)** *Application/Commentary.* One main idea of the article is that country music is changing in a positive manner and that more people are enjoying it. This idea is reflected in both parts of the title. (2), (3), and (4) are the opposite of what is suggested. (5) refers to a show mentioned only as a contrasting example.

6. **(4)** *Literal Comprehension/Commentary.* Lardner's characters are described as shallow, lying, and cheap (lines 6–8); unloving and cruel (lines 10–18); and loud, wretched, crooked, stupid, and desperate (lines 39–42). Of the choices given, only "horrible" fits this picture of humanity.

7. **(1)** *Inferential Comprehension/Commentary.* Kazin said that Lardner's work had a "harsh, glazed coldness." Kazin saw much pessimism in Lardner's writing. This view is supported by the context in which this quotation is placed—a context that speaks of Lardner's "brutal" stories, his "grim realism" and "his dreadful events."

8. **(5)** *Literal Comprehension/Commentary.* The view of Lardner as a mystery is stated in lines 39–40. The author's personality appears to contain many contradictions. (1) is an overstatement of Lardner's drinking. The other choices refer to the characters in Lardner's fiction.

9. **(1)** *Analysis/Commentary.* The comparison is a strongly negative image, thus eliminating (2), (3), and (4). It focuses not on Lardner's style (5) but on his content. It implies that the "dreadful events" in Lardner's fiction and insecticide have something in common. Since insecticide is a poison, it can be assumed that there is something deadly about Lardner's work, too.

10. **(4)** *Application/Commentary.* The reviewer seems to dislike the grim, gruesome, and depressing. A program about a serial killer would most likely focus on the dark side of human nature. This reviewer would probably prefer any of the other choices.

11. **(2)** *Literal Comprehension/Commentary.* The author's view of Rockwell as a sentimental painter begins with a reference to Rockwell's "trust in his own and American sentiment" (lines 3–4). The author goes on to speak of the "filter of sentiment" in Rockwell's work and how that quality is what divides people's opinions about the painter's art (lines 29–33). The "sentimentality" is the focus of the entire passage.

12. **(1)** *Literal Comprehension/Commentary.* According to the author, Rockwell's technique is "the most perfect where is dissolves, imperceptibly, into anecdote" (lines 7–8).

13. **(3)** *Inferential Comprehension/ Commentary.* The examples of Rockwell's subjects are things that Americans would see all around them. His portrayal of the familiar and simple things of life would have appealed to most people. Rather than being challenging (1), his painting were comforting. The other choices would not have influenced the general public.

14. **(5)** *Analysis/Commentary.* The author describes Rockwell's work as "unadorned" (line 12), thus eliminating (3). Of the choices given, only (5) appears in the passage. In lines 20–26, the author names the subjects of four famous Rockwell paintings. He uses these examples to illustrate his belief that this is the view of America that Rockwell saw and re-created in his works—his "photographically convincing portrayal of *real* life (lines 12–14).

15. **(4)** *Analysis/Commentary.* The imagined conversation that the author presents is a discussion in which young art students and their parents cannot understand each other's opinions of Rockwell. By describing this scene, the author provides a vivid illustration of how strongly people feel about Rockwell—and how strongly they can disagree over the value of his work.

16. **(3)** *Literal Comprehension/Commentary.* After noting that the death of American movies has been announced "many times before" (lines 1–2), the author mentions that Pauline Kael had made just such an announcement "six years ago" (line 18). All of the other announcements that the author mentions occurred earlier (lines 2–14).

17. **(1)** *Inferential Comprehension/ Commentary.* The author says that he has "many new reasons to be gloomy about the studios" (lines 28–29) and that American movies "have become an object of contempt" (lines 41–43). He then goes on to argue that most people feel that movies have been "trivialized...and marketed to death" (lines 46–48). It can be assumed from this evidence that the author is pessimistic about the future of American movies.

18. **(5)** *Inferential Comprehension/ Commentary.* The discussion of movie criticism indicates that the reviewer is quite familiar with the history of the industry. There is no suggestion to support any of the other choices.

19. **(3)** *Application/Commentary.* The author describes recent American movies as "trivialized, infantilized, massified, and marketed to death" (lines 46–48). He concludes the passage by stating, "At the moment, the only thing the system does well is market" (lines 58–60). With such strong references to mass-market appeal and to marketing in general, it seems likely that he would agree with a comparison between the movie and advertising industries.

20. **(2)** *Analysis/Commentary.* Quoting another film critic who agrees with his negative view of current American movies is a good way for the author to strengthen his argument.

21. **(2)** *Literal Comprehension/Commentary.* After stating in paragraph one that the quality of most television "entertainments" is "low," the author goes on to argue that the public "wants more," and that many people "consistently ask for programs of a higher intellectual content."

22. **(1)** *Inferential Comprehension/ Commentary.* Since the Ford anniversary show omitted the New Deal entirely, even though it did deal with strikes and the Depression, you can infer that the word "intractable" means difficult to manage or manipulate.

23. **(2)** *Application/Commentary.* Fast-food restaurants, like the anniversary show, are successful because of a conditioning process. People have been convinced that fast-food provides a satisfying alternative to regular meals. This process is similar to the way TV persuades the audience that the programs are what is wanted by the public. The same process is not involved with the success of the other choices.

24. **(5)** *Analysis/Commentary.* By comparing the Ford anniversary show version of American history to unsophisticated, slapstick entertainment—"vaudeville"—the author conveys the idea that the show trivialized American history.

25. **(5)** *Inferential Comprehension/ Commentary.* The reviewer states that the mass media provides entertainment (2), thrills (1), and laughs (4). Despite its lack of quality, the anniversary show was historically based (3). What is missing, even to the audience's mind (lines 33–34), is a selection of serious programs.

26. **(4)** *Literal Comprehension/Commentary.* Although (2) is mentioned and (3) is implied, the main topic of the passage is the new McDonald's in Berwyn, Illinois—a McDonald's with a bold, innovative design.

27. **(2)** *Inferential Comprehension/Commentary.* The "gray-flannel architecture profession" is contrasted with SITE, whose designs are "notorious for radical reversals." The author says that SITE "strikes fear in the heart" of the "gray-flannel" group. Since a "radical" firm would be most likely to upset a conservative or stuffy establishment, it can be assumed that the term "gray-flannel" means "conservative."

28. **(2)** *Inferential Comprehension/Commentary.* The new McDonald's is described in lines 30–43. The description includes terms such as "poised for flight" (lines 34–35) and "floats weightlessly" (line 35). Mention of the building materials focuses on glass. Of the choices given, "airy" (2) best summarizes the description.

29. **(1)** *Literal Comprehension/Commentary.* The mall owner, David Bermant, was the person who first requested "a more daring design" (lines 18–19). (2), (3), and (4) refer to the designers who worked on the project. McDonald's (5) only responded to Bermant's challenge; the company did not come up with the idea.

30. **(3)** *Application/Commentary.* What the author seems to appreciate most is that this new McDonald's serves its purpose yet looks beautiful. He concludes, "For the first time, McDonald's is a magnet for devotees of architecture as well as of hamburgers" (lines 46–48). It could be expected that he might want to see the same mix of visual appeal and function in his own home.

31. **(2)** *Literal Comprehension/Commentary.* The city, Cairo, is mentioned in line 4. The country, Egypt, is mentioned in line 42. London (1) is the site of Dickens' novels. The tea gardens near the Nile (3) is where the author, Mahfouz, relaxes. An Egyptian newspaper office (4) is where the author works, not where the novel is set. The mind of the novel's central character, the mother, does not include all the action of the novel; so (5) is wrong.

32. **(4)** *Literal Comprehension/Commentary.* Religious zealots were angered, rather than pleased, by Mahfouz's work. All the other choices are stated as true about the author.

33. **(4)** *Inferential Comprehension/Commentary.* Mahfouz is sought out because of his fame. He even states that he has become a "prisoner of the prize" (lines 82–83), referring to the attention the Nobel Prize has brought him. The journalists and scholars are not connected to the threats against his life (1). There is no suggestion of a connection between the other choices and the requests for interviews.

34. **(2)** *Analysis/Commentary.* The first and last paragraphs tell the reader about the author's background and his present life. They act to frame the discussion of the novel itself. Even though they are about the author, they are not intended to promote autobiographies or explain Mahfouz's motivation, eliminating (1) and (3). Neither (4) nor (5) is connected to the framing paragraphs.

35. **(2)** *Application/Commentary.* Based on the reviewer's comments about the importance of the family in Egypt and on the contents of Mahfouz's novel, Mahfouz sees the family as fundamental. The contents of his novel suggest that he would disagree with (1), (3), and (4). The problems Mahfouz has encountered indicate that religion plays an important part in the life of Egypt (5).

36. **(4)** *Literal Comprehension/Commentary.* Although the reviewer enjoyed the movie remake (2), he states that he had "no inclination to watch" (lines 24–25) the series after seeing one episode. Part of his explanation includes his dislike of the changes (3).

37. **(2)** *Inferential Comprehension/Commentary.* The reviewer's references to the original show demonstrate his familiarity with and fondness for the show. He sounds as though he had been a regular viewer, so (1) and (4) are wrong. The reviewer implies that, even though he enjoys vampire-based shows, he does not necessarily like them all (3). There is no suggestion of (5).

38. **(1)** *Application/Commentary.* Based on the author's enjoyment of the trappings of the vampire movie, he would want characters to be spooky. He also states that the program was not goofy enough (line 54). The reviewer enjoyed

the dual and surprising roles of the seventh episode (2) but not the modern touches (4) or unbelievable actions of the police (5).

39. **(1)** *Analysis/Commentary.* The reviewer's word choice is drawn from images associated with vampires. By substituting these puns for more ordinary phrases, he adds a light-hearted note to the article. The other four choices are not adequate explanations of his word choice.

40. **(4)** *Application/Commentary.* The reviewer probably was sad that the remake of the series didn't work. But he seems to expect its failure. He would neither want it renewed (1) and (2), rejoice in its end (3), nor be totally indifferent (5). His reaction probably would be expressed in a vampire-related pun.

Half-length Practice Test

1. **(3)** *Literal Comprehension/Fiction.* The speaker says of herself, "... the reason I was hardly in a position to date...was that I was seven months pregnant" (lines 14–17).

2. **(2)** *Inferential Comprehension/Fiction.* Although there are elements of humor in the passage, the speaker indicates that she is upset with comments such as "I was crying most of the time" (lines 21–22) and her detailed disgust upon finding the inscribed book of children's songs (lines 27–37).

3. **(3)** *Application/Fiction.* When the speaker discovered the bad news of her husband's betrayal, she immediately took a flight to New York (lines 27–28)—a rather emotional act. Her bitter, mocking anger indicates that her emotional reaction to the news was not cautious, thus eliminating (1), or reserved in any other fashion, thus eliminating (2), (4), and (5). If her boss gave her the bad news that she was fired, she might be expected to act emotionally and probably impulsively.

4. **(1)** *Analysis/Fiction.* Although the speaker has good reason to be upset, she writes in a light, informal manner. The jokes she makes along the way, such as her discussion of the word *date* (lines 9–20) and her description of Thelma Rice (lines 39–43), help to create a humorous tone.

5. **(1)** *Inferential Comprehension/Nonfiction.* The description indicates that Mrs. Flowers stands apart from most of the community. The narrator mentions that she always looks cool when others are warm (lines 2–6), she wears voile like others wear denim (lines 8–10), and she has ice when others do not (lines 19–24). These details suggest Mrs. Flowers' refinement. More important, however, is the impression that she makes upon the narrator when reading *A Tale of Two Cities* (lines 38–54). She impresses the narrator by making the words sound more beautiful than the narrator could have imagined.

6. **(4)** *Inferential Comprehension/Nonfiction.* It is the sound of Mrs. Flowers' voice that fascinates the narrator. In lines 45–54, she describes the musical quality but says that she hadn't heard a word. This experience does not affect her career decisions (1) or her understanding of literature or music (3) and (5). She had already enjoyed the book as a romantic novel when she had read it to herself (2).

7. **(3)** *Inferential Comprehension/Nonfiction.* The speaker's early description of Mrs. Flowers as someone who had "grace of control" and a "private breeze which swirled around" her shows that the speaker is impressed with Mrs. Flowers. Later, she discusses how Mrs. Flowers encouraged her with her "lessons in living." Finally, when Mrs. Flowers reads to her, the speaker says that she "heard poetry for the first time in my life." All of these details points out how much the speaker admires Mrs. Flowers.

8. **(3)** *Analysis/Nonfiction.* From the point of view of the black community, a rich white woman would have been seen as socially powerful. By comparing Mrs. Flowers to this type of figure, the author indicates the importance of Mrs. Flowers within the black community. The other choices do not relate to the woman's importance.

9. **(4)** *Literal Comprehension/Drama.* Frankie refers several times in the passage to her brother's wedding and mentions "the bride and my brother" (lines 54–55) and "my brother and the bride" (line 58).

10. **(1)** *Inferential Comprehension/Drama.* Twice (lines 33–36 and 59–60) Frankie says that she will go with her brother and his bride to Winter Hill, suggesting that Winter Hill is their new home.

11. **(3)** *Analysis/Drama.* When John Henry suggests to Frankie that they go play with the children (lines 27–28), Frankie talks instead about an important step she plans to take in her life. By having the noise of the children

"(*in the distance*)" (stage direction, lines 25–26), the author is able to show that Frankie is moving out of childhood and becoming an adult.

12. **(1)** *Application/Drama.* Frankie sees nothing wrong with joining the bride and groom after the wedding. She does not see herself as intruding on their privacy. Family (2) and belonging (3) are very important to Frankie. Based on her experience in lines 54–55, she would be likely to agree with (4) and (5).
13. **(5)** *Literal Comprehension/Commentary.* In lines 4–10, the author lists five characteristics that great actors possess, ending with "the ability to communicate a sense of danger." He begins the next sentence by agreeing that these characteristics have many orders of importance but that he feels that "the last attribute is surely the rarest" (lines 14–15).
14. **(2)** *Inferential Comprehension/Commentary.* The author states throughout the passage that Olivier is very different from the average actor because of his "splendid fury" (line 26). He also says that when Olivier tries to play a "common man" role, "He seldom succeeds" (line 48).
15. **(4)** *Application/Commentary.* The author suggests that Olivier is at his best when he is playing "the exceptional characters around whom playwrights of the past built their tallest tragedies and highest comedies" (lines 55–58). Of the choices given, only the plays of Shakespeare fit this description. It is quite likely that in all of the other choices, Olivier would be asked to play a "common man"—the kind of role in which Olivier "bursts the seams" (lines 50–51).
16. **(1)** *Analysis/Commentary.* The author is using figurative language to say that Olivier believes his eyes are his best feature. The comparison is to a winning card. The comparison is not negative as suggested by (2).
17. **(3)** *Analysis/Commentary.* Earlier in the passage the author speaks of Olivier's "vein of rage" (line 22) and says that a "volcano remains active" in him (lines 34–35). Comparing Olivier to an "internal combustion engine" is a way of further emphasizing his power as a dramatic actor. The other choices may be true of Olivier as an actor, but they are not discussed in the passage.
18. **(2)** *Literal Comprehension/Fiction.* The relationship between the two speakers is established when Daisy says to Nick, "We don't know each other very well...Even if we are cousins" (lines 8–10).
19. **(1)** *Literal Comprehension/Fiction.* Daisy tells Nick that she is glad to have a daughter. She adds, "And I hope she'll be a fool—that's the best thing a girl can be in this world, a beautiful little fool" (lines 34–36).
20. **(4)** *Inferential Comprehension/Fiction.* At this point in the passage, Daisy is described as defiant and full of scorn (lines 43–44). After she has made the statement, Nick realizes that she is not sincere (lines 51–53). Based on these details, (4) offers the best explanation of Daisy's statement.
21. **(3)** *Literal Comprehension/Poetry.* After naming several possible reasons why one might become a wartime flyer, the speaker says that it was "A lonely impulse of delight" (line 11)—in other words, merely a whim—that brought him to his place in the military.
22. **(1)** *Inferential Comprehension/Poetry.* The speaker makes no mention of a mother (5) or a sweetheart (4). From his statement "Those that I guard I do not love" (line 4) it seems that he does not have a strong sense of patriotism for Ireland as a nation (1). His general attitude throughout the poem is one of indifference, even to his own fate (3). The only strength of feeling seems to come when he refers to Kiltartan Cross as "My country" (line 5) and its people as "My countrymen" (line 6).
23. **(2)** *Analysis/Poetry.* The unemotional word choice in this poem, which appears from the beginning "I know that I shall meet my fate" (line 1), creates a tone of acceptance and resignation.

Full-length Practice Test

1. **(4)** *Inferential Comprehension/Fiction.* The anger and cruelty in José Montiel is seen most dramatically in the way he grabs his son roughly and tries to force an explanation out of him (lines 29–31). Further on, the author refers to his emotion at that point as "fury" (line 36). Later in the passage, that fury appears again when José Montiel becomes enraged at Balthazar, despite the presence of a crowd (lines 58–62). Some of the qualities named in the other choices might be appropriate (especially "firm," "egotistical," and "foolish"); only in (4), however, are both characteristics appropriate.
2. **(3)** *Literal Comprehension/Fiction.* The passage begins "Balthazar was no stranger to José Montiel's house" (lines 1–2) and concludes "The last thing we need is for some nobody to give orders

in my house" (lines 64–66). Nothing in the passage suggests a change of scene. Furthermore, the casual appearance of José Montiel (lines 13–15) and the way in which he freely argues with his son in the presence of Balthazar suggest that he feels at home here.

3. **(2)** *Inferential Comprehension/Fiction.* Although José Montiel becomes angry earlier in the passage, his anger is directed at Balthazar only after Balthazar gives Pepe the cage as a gift, thus eliminating (1) and (3). By making the boy happy, Balthazar has ignored José Montiel's authority. Furthermore, he does it without losing face himself and in front of many witnesses. José Montiel's anger at this point is largely humiliation. There is no evidence in the passage to support (4) or (5).
4. **(3)** *Inferential Comprehension/Fiction.* The woman speaks her husband's name as if trying to distract him from his anger. Her whisper further suggests that she would prefer a quiet resolution to the incident. There is no evidence that she is taking anyone's side, thus eliminating (1), (4) and (5). Her whispering voice does not express anger (2).
5. **(4)** *Application/Fiction.* Balthazar's discomfort is mentioned at the beginning of the passage. What happens after that—namely, his conversation with José Montiel—eliminates (1), (3), and (5). In that exchange, Balthazar has shown that he can stand up to the wealthy. In the future, therefore, it does not seem likely that he will fear them again. (2) might be considered, but the way in which Balthazar speaks and acts indicates that he would work on the basis of a verbal agreement.
6. **(3)** *Literal Comprehension/Nonfiction.* Of her and her brother's movie-going, the author says, "We went three and four afternoons a week" (lines 21–22).
7. **(5)** *Inferential Comprehension/Nonfiction.* The author does not mention John Wayne's physical strength (1), his good looks (2), or his brilliance as an actor (4). She does mention the way he walked (3), but what has stayed in her mind and shaped her views is the romantic promise he made to a girl in *War of the Wildcats*, (lines 27–31).
8. **(1)** *Application/Nonfiction.* The author's point in this passage is that romantic fantasies have played an important part in her life, thus eliminating (2), but that they do not—or perhaps cannot—come true, thus eliminating (3) and (5). Real life seems to be something of a disappointment for the author, thus eliminating (4). Her memories of the past are special to her, but she is still looking for that kind of happiness in the present.
9. **(2)** *Analysis/Nonfiction.* The author associates "artificial rain" (lines 16–17) with her childhood. In the conclusion of the passage, she is talking about that part of her that once was a child. It is meant as a sign of hope, thus eliminating the other choices.
10. **(2)** *Inferential Comprehension/Drama.* The conversation between Lennie and George indicates that they travel around together and work at a variety of temporary jobs. Together they look toward the day when they can settle down.
11. **(4)** *Literal Comprehension/Drama.* Throughout the passage, Lennie urges George to tell him again about what they will do someday. The other topics are mentioned during the course of the conversation, but it is the idea of settling down that receives the most attention.
12. **(3)** *Analysis/Drama.* The way in which Lennie interrupts George makes him seem almost childlike in his excitement. Childlike excitement would be an appealing quality for most audiences, and they probably would take Lennie's part in any future conflict with George, based on what they have seen of Lennie here.
13. **(5)** *Literal Comprehension/Drama.* George states that ranch hands "don't belong no place" (lines 20–21). He does not seem to believe any of the other choices.
14. **(5)** *Literal Comprehension/Commentary.* The author says that modern comedies do not make people laugh as hard as they used to and that over time, screen quality "has quietly but steadily deteriorated" (lines 34–35). This lack of "old-time humor" in more recent comedies is the topic of the entire passage.
15. **(3)** *Literal Comprehension/Commentary.* In lines 41–67, the author provides a detailed contrast between the way a modern comedian and a silent-screen comedian would react to a hit on the head. Both kinds of comedians would faint, he says, but the silent-screen comedian would do it in a much funnier way.
16. **(3)** *Application/Commentary.* Based on the author's praise of silent movies and the elaborate sight gags of silent comedians, it is likely that he would prefer a

modern comedy that employed sight gags. None of the other choices involve a lot of visual stimulation. Their focus is on the verbal or auditory.

17. **(4)** *Analysis/Commentary.* After describing the four kinds of laughter, the author goes on to explain how many of these kinds of laughter comedies should be able to produce. His purpose, then, is to introduce his belief that the best comedies can produce all four kinds of laughter.

18. **(2)** *Analysis/Commentary.* Whips and ladders are usually associated with animal acts in a circus. By using these terms in the context of comedy, the author stresses that good comedians should be skillful enough to have complete control over their audience.

19. **(4)** *Literal Comprehension/Poetry.* In the first stanza the speaker says, "Across the street he stood," when talking about the clarinet player. Later, the speaker talks about "the one man band/By the quick lunch stand." This indicates that the clarinet player is performing in the street.

20. **(1)** *Inferential Comprehension/Poetry.* Since the speaker "plays" for "fortune" and is used to getting "velvet curtain calls," you can infer that she is a successful, well-known musician.

21. **(3)** *Analysis/Poetry.* The speaker seems to be intrigued by, and respectful of, the clarinet player. She seems almost ashamed of their differences. By repeating several times that the clarinet player performs "for free," the poet emphasizes the contrast between him and the musician who plays "for fortune."

22. **(3)** *Literal Comprehension/Poetry.* Lines 22 to 24 state the reason. He had never been on TV, so the people passed him by.

23. **(5)** *Literal Comprehension/Fiction.* In lines 16–17 Eleanor says: "You look down on me... I know you do. I can tell." This means that she feels he does not respect her enough. None of the other choices accurately describe the attitude she expresses in these lines.

24. **(2)** *Inferential Comprehension/Fiction.* Both terms of each choice must fit the characters to be accurate. The two people are experiencing passionate attraction and liking for each other, but at the same time each of them expresses doubt as to whether the other person really likes and respects her or him. (Eleanor expresses this doubt in lines 16–17 and the narrator expresses his doubt about her feelings for him in lines 31–34.) This question also might be answered by eliminating the choices that clearly do not describe the characters. Because of their doubts they are not "carefree" (3), and though they are nervous, somewhat frightened, and are certainly excited, they are not depressed or angry, so (1) and (5) are wrong.

25. **(1)** *Application/Fiction.* In lines 2–6 the narrator expresses wonder by saying "I hadn't known I could feel like this," and compares his feeling to "an enormous meadow,"; he says " It seemed to me a miracle that human beings could be so elaborate." The narrator's long passionate kiss at the end of the passage gives him intense pleasure and pain simultaneously. Eleanor is crying in lines 10–11 but seems happy during the rest of the passage. Their happiness does not die down because they kiss passionately at the end, so (2) is wrong. Both are insecure but their self-doubts do not destroy their positive experience (3). The narrator does communicate his feelings to Eleanor ("I think you're wonderful!"—lines 13–14), so (4) is wrong. They experience more joy than pain, so (5) is incorrect.

26. **(4)** *Analysis/Fiction.* Eleanor talks about geometry right after the narrator says: "We were standing very close to one another. We talked industriously." "Industriously" indicates they are working hard to make conversation because they are "very close" and need to reduce the tension of their new intimacy. Though (1) might seem correct, Eleanor has just assured him that she does not think he is "second-best," so at this point in the passage he is the insecure one, not herself; therefore, her motive more likely would be to make the narrator feel intelligent. However, her talk about geometry does not suggest in any way that she thinks he is smart in math. She is just making conversation to reduce the tension of their new intimacy. Nothing Eleanor says or does suggests the meanings stated in the other choices.

27. **(4)** *Literal Comprehension/Drama.* The passage begins with Elwood's explanation of how he met Harvey. His story begins with "I had just helped Ed Hickey into a taxi" (lines 1–2). It is as he walks away from that event that he notices Harvey watching him.

28. **(3)** *Inferential Comprehension/Drama.* If Dr. Sanderson believed Elwood's story, he would be asking Elwood more questions about Harvey. Instead, he tries to find out why Elwood cares so much about the name "Harvey." That detail—which takes up most of the conversation in the passage—indicates that the doctor does not believe that Harvey the rabbit actually exists.

29. **(4)** *Inferential Comprehension/Drama.* The doctor is clearly concerned about Elwood's mental processes. Elwood is not, so (3) is eliminated. Elwood does not seem worried about Ed Hickey (1), nor is there a suggestion that Harvey is ill (2). There is no support for (5). These ideas, combined with Elwood's unusual story, lead to the inference in (4).

30. **(3)** *Analysis/Drama.* Elwood never speaks directly to Harvey in this passage. Dr. Sanderson's persistent questioning indicates his frustration (1), which becomes more and more humorous as Elwood persists in answering with perfect calmness (4). The topic of the conversation—"a great white rabbit" (line 7)—*is* ridiculous (2). Elwood's explanation of his hopes for the name—that he never knew anyone else with that name (lines 53–54)—is funny, too.

31. **(4)** *Literal Comprehension/Nonfiction.* Lines 11 to 19 describe the location of the dump in reference to the town and other landmarks. (1), (2), and (5) are eliminated because the dump is in the southeast corner of town. The Alph River (3) is at the end of a system of rivers, not near the town. But the river that passed the dump was also near a "campsite for passing teamsters, gypsies, sometimes Indians" (lines 23–24).

32. **(1)** *Literal Comprehension/Nonfiction.* The author says that a spot near the dump was the "favorite campsite for passing teamsters, gypsies, sometimes Indians." He then refers to these people as "migrant tenants," indicating that the word "migrant" means wandering.

33. **(3)** *Inferential Comprehension/Nonfiction.* The fact that the author looked at the dump as a place of "adventure" and thought a buckle he found there might be gold suggests that he was still a child when he lived in Whitemud.

34. **(2)** *Application/Nonfiction.* The author uses words like "poetry," "excitement," "adventure," and "wonder" to convey his feelings about the dump. Consequently, he would probably choose the phrase "a magic kingdom" to describe how he once felt about the dump.

35. **(5)** *Analysis/Nonfiction.* Since artifacts are the objects that are found at archaeological sites, the author uses that word to stress how much the camps were like those sites.

36. **(5)** *Literal Comprehension/Poetry.* The speaker refers to the sea (lines 2 and 14), fishermen (line 5), sailors (line 7), the bay (line 8), and ships (line 9)—all images concerned with the ocean.

37. **(4)** *Inferential Comprehension/Poetry.* The thought in lines 11–12 is connected with the thought in lines 15–16. Both suggest a parting that is final—especially the words "vanished" (line 11) and the expression "a day that is dead" (line 15).

38. **(2)** *Analysis/Poetry.* The rhythm in these lines is so strong and regular that it sounds like ocean waves. The rhythm speaks of the power of the sea, but it does not directly link the power of the sea to death itself.

39. **(2)** *Analysis/Poetry.* The "O" is an exclamation in itself. Combined with the exclamation point, it adds to the sense of emotional involvement. The "O" does not function in any of the other suggested ways.

40. **(4)** *Literal Comprehension/Commentary.* The author focuses most of the second paragraph on the question of style reflecting character and even says, "*Style is character.*"

41. **(1)** *Inferential Comprehension/Commentary.* Georgia O'Keeffe herself indicated that people should pay attention to her art, not her life, so (4) is wrong. This suggests that people do pay attention to how she has lived. The author provides hints of what may fascinate others by mentioning the Stieglitz photos and O'Keeffe's living arrangements. She is clearly the opposite of uninteresting (2). The author appears only to have read about the artist, not to have known her (5).

42. **(2)** *Inferential Comprehension/Commentary.* The author talks in the second paragraph about style illustrating character. When she says that "every choice one made alone... betrayed one's character," therefore, she implies that the word "betrayed" means "revealed" in this context.

43. **(2)** *Application / Commentary.* Since the author believes that, in any form of art, style is character, she would probably say that listening to many works of music by the same composer will reveal something about that composer's personality.

44. **(3)** *Analysis / Commentary.* An effective picture of sky and clouds would suggest a sense of airiness and floating. The author uses the word "floated" to stress how well O'Keeffe's painting, "Sky Above Clouds," captures a sense of the sky.

45. **(5)** *Analysis / Commentary.* The author originally describes O'Keeffe's painting as "vast" but stresses its size at the end of the passage by referring to the "192 square feet" of the painting.

Simulated Test

1. **(5)** *Literal Comprehension / Fiction.* It is said that Walter Mitty hates the weekly trips to Waterbury because "he was always getting something wrong" (lines 8–9). In the first paragraph of the passage, Walter mentally reviews a list of drugstore articles; in the third paragraph, he remembers a supermarket item.

2. **(2)** *Inferential Comprehension / Fiction.* The courtroom scene appears right after Walter Mitty hears a newsboy shouting a headline about a trial. It ends when "the buildings of Waterbury rose up out of the misty courtroom" (lines 44–46). These details suggest the unreality of the scene—that the courtroom scene takes place only in Walter Mitty's mind. There is no mention of television (1) or novels (5) in the passage.

3. **(4)** *Application / Fiction.* What is memorable about the character of Walter Mitty is his habit of slipping into a fantasy world in which he plays dramatic, heroic characters. (1), (3), and (5) are examples of such fantasies. (2) fits his characteristic of forgetfulness about small details. Based on information in the passage, (4) would be the least likely choice; if Walter Mitty heard about a tragic accident, he probably would imagine himself in a fantasy in which he could save those involved.

4. **(1)** *Analysis / Fiction.* In this passage, there is no physical description of Mrs. Mitty (3), nor does the passage conclude with a surprise (5). The implied contrast between Walter Mitty and his wife (2) is a minor detail. Walter Mitty's actions in the fantasy courtroom (4) are humorous details, but they are only part of the larger source of humor, the contrast between Walter Mitty's bold fantasies and his unremarkable real life.

5. **(3)** *Literal Comprehension / Nonfiction.* The author describes Stretch's general appearance and health (1), devotes a paragraph to what Stretch thinks of doctors (2), describes much of his daily activity (4), and how his feet affect his walk (5). But the only mention of business is "his shop" (line 42). There is no description of what business it is.

6. **(4)** *Literal Comprehension / Nonfiction.* The author states in lines 3–4 that his doctors have told him not to drink or smoke. But in lines 30–33 the author says he smokes strong cigarettes and has a few drinks every day.

7. **(3)** *Inferential Comprehension / Nonfiction.* Stretch is supporting his own position by referring to a well-known figure who was also lectured by his doctors but lived a long time. Churchill ignored them for twenty years, so Stretch thinks his doctor's warning that he has only six or seven years to live is foolish. He is supplying evidence that contradicts (1). Stretch doesn't seem the type who would need to impress anyone (4). Choices (2) and (5) don't really fit the example.

8. **(5)** *Analysis / Nonfiction.* Stretch is obviously in pain from his feet. But he is incredibly active despite the problem. By detailing the foot problem, the author provides impressive evidence for his statement that Stretch has an enormous amount of energy for a man of his age in his condition. There is no support for (1). (2) is based on Stretch's joke, not on reality. The reader may feel sympathy for Stretch (4), but the details are presented in a way that encourage respect more than sympathy.

9. **(1)** *Application / Nonfiction.* As he is presented in this passage, Stretch does not sound like a man who would complain about a minor ache. He would, if anything, make a joke of it (2). Based on the information about his energy, it would not be surprising if Stretch continued to be active (4 and 5) after work.

10. **(3)** *Literal Comprehension / Commentary.* The reviewer praises the acting ability of everyone in the cast, although he says of Joseph Wiseman that he "is a bit too pat as the unfeeling father."

11. **(2)** *Inferential Comprehension/ Commentary.* The author writes that Robin Williams gives the "best dramatic performance of his career" and refers to previous performances as "mechanical and pinched," and such a performance could not have been very convincing. The author does not suggest that Williams' performance is humorous, so (3) is eliminated. Even though the author describes Williams' performance as serious, he does not suggest that it was intended to be humorous. Therefore, (4) is also eliminated.

12. **(2)** *Inferential Comprehension/ Commentary.* By saying that these filmmakers went beyond a simple moving of the novel's contents into a film script, the author implies that this is not always the case. The suggestion is that a successful film adaptation requires additional creativity.

13. **(2)** *Application/Commentary.* The review opens with a description of Tommy's string of bad luck and, later, stresses Tommy's sense of desperation and panic. Since the program is about Tommy's mounting troubles, it is unlikely that he will experience positive things.

14. **(4)** *Analysis/Commentary.* The opening paragraph quickly and dramatically describes the plight of the film's main character. A description of a man "on the verge of losing his mind" might grab a reader's interest in the rest of the article and in the film itself. It is doubtful that the producers would make a film that required something to be read to understand it, so (1) is eliminated. None of the author's own feelings about the film are expressed in the opening paragraph, so (2), (3), and (5) also must be eliminated.

15. **(2)** *Analysis/Commentary.* The reference to Bellow as the author of the novel on which the film is based establishes the quality of the source because Bellow has both "widespread acclaim" and has been a winner of the Nobel Prize (lines 19–20).

16. **(2)** *Inferential Comprehension/Poetry.* The speaker presents positive images of her grandmothers, thus eliminating (1), (3), and (5). They were strong, sturdy, hard-working, and full of songs and memories. She takes them quite seriously, for she wants to be like them, thus eliminating (4). The attitude of awe is seen especially in her comment, "They touched earth and grain grew" (line 4).

17. **(4)** *Literal Comprehension/Poetry.* Of herself, the speaker asks, "Why am I not as they?" (line 12). She compares herself to her grandmothers, thus eliminating (1), (2), and (5). Rather than speaking of how they have aged (3), she speaks of their strength and their "clean words" (line 10). These are virtues that she wishes she saw more of in herself.

18. **(3)** *Application/Poetry.* The speaker values her grandmothers' strength and their "clean words"—the things they have to say. In another setting, the speaker would want to make use of these virtues. Of the choices given, (1) and (5) would shut such people away, where what they had to offer could not be used. (2) has no direct bearing on the question. (4) would not allow such people to continue to be productive; (3), however, would make it possible for such people to offer their strength and their "clean words" to the next generation in a more far-reaching way.

19. **(5)** *Inferential Comprehension/Fiction.* The details in the passage indicate that there are different sets of rules for whites and blacks, eliminating (3) and (4). The man says, "There are benches down there for you!" People are surprised by the sight of "a black man sitting on a white man's bench." Since the man calls a policeman to get Karlie off the bench, it can be assumed that the law supports these different sets of rights, eliminating (2). Though there is violence and fighting, nowhere is it suggested that the people enjoy it, eliminating (1).

20. **(1)** *Inferential Comprehension/Fiction.* Karlie is challenged when he is sitting on a bench upon which he is not supposed to sit. Karlie feels that he might have won when the first challenger seems to back down in the "bench dispute" (lines 23–24). When he is arrested for sitting on the bench, he feels that he definitely has won (lines 59–60).

21. **(2)** *Literal Comprehension/Fiction.* At the end of the passage, Karlie relaxes from his resistance. Speaking Karlie's thoughts, the author says, "It was useless fighting any longer...He had challenged and won" (lines 58–61).

22. **(5)** *Analysis/Fiction.* The detailed descriptions that the author uses increase the readers' sense of reality of the passage. The details help the reader

imagine that he or she is there, experiencing the sights and sounds that the characters are experiencing.

23. **(3)** *Analysis/Fiction.* The words spoken by the boy create an image of an aggressive white person. The author also provides description of his voice (line 2), eyes (line 6), and his race and age (line 22). Neither (4) nor (5) adds to the image of the boy.

24. **(3)** *Literal Comprehension/Nonfiction.* The author saw this battle "when I went out to my wood-pile" (lines 1–2). He is surprised "to find that the chips were covered" with fighting ants (lines 8–11). He spends the rest of the passage describing the event he witnessed there.

25. **(4)** *Inferential Comprehension/Nonfiction.* The author says he is surprised to find a full-scale battle at his feet (lines 10–12). Then he states that it was the only battlefield he had been on while the battle was in progress (lines 17–21). This appears to be the reason he is drawn into watching.

26. **(3)** *Inferential Comprehension/Nonfiction.* The author describes the ants as fierce (line 4), persistent (lines 6–8 and 38), resolute (line 27), and unwilling to surrender (lines 31–32, and 39–41). There is no caution (1) or fear (4) indicated in the way they fight. Some observers might consider them brave (2), but the author is most impressed by their savagery.

27. **(2)** *Analysis/Nonfiction.* The author refers to the ants as "combatants" (line 9) and as "republicans" and "imperialists" (lines 20–21). All of the choices given refer to techniques that the author uses, but only (2) refers to a technique that is used specifically to compare ants with people.

28. **(4)** *Literal Comprehension/Drama.* In lines 22–30, Annie names three advantages that she would have as a teacher: (1) she has read everything that Dr. Howe, an expert, has written; (2) she is full of youthful energy; and (3) she has been blind herself and thus knows the problems that a blind student would face.

29. **(3)** *Inferential Comprehension/Drama.* At first, Kate is doubtful about Annie's qualifications. But as Annie answers her questions, Kate becomes more accepting of Annie's knowledge. By the last speech, Kate appears to believe Annie is qualified and even reassures the woman about her worth. Kate has begun to believe the child can be helped, as opposed to (4), but does not expect miracles (5).

30. **(2)** *Inferential Comprehension/Drama.* Annie makes this statement in response to Kate's question about what she thinks is the first or most important thing to teach. If language were *exactly* to the mind what light is to the eye, then language would be connected with the ability to speak as light is connected with the ability to see. Annie, however, says that it offers *more* than that, as if it were a basic key to understanding things.

31. **(5)** *Analysis/Drama.* When real people speak, they don't always use complete sentences. The author wants his characters to sound real, so he has them speak in incomplete sentences at times, too. Using occasional incomplete sentences does not make a character ill-educated (1) or tense (2). Though there is warmth between Annie and Kate, the incomplete sentences do not help create it, eliminating (3). Incomplete sentences would not make the dialogue easier to memorize, so (4) is also eliminated.

32. **(4)** *Literal Comprehension/Nonfiction.* The author introduces the topic—the ratio of brain size to body size for dinosaurs—in lines 20–21. In lines 1–20, he leads up to this point; in the rest of the passage, he defends it.

33. **(1)** *Inferential Comprehension/Nonfiction.* In describing "paleontologists" as thinkers (lines 3–5 and 12–14), the author indicates that they are people, thus eliminating (2), (3), and (4); who live in the present, thus eliminating (5). Their special field of interest is dinosaurs, which indicates that they are scientists.

34. **(3)** *Application/Nonfiction.* The author does not address the question of why the dinosaur disappeared; rather, he addresses the question of their alleged stupidity. He concludes that "large ani-

mals require relatively less brain to do as well as smaller animals" (lines 47–49). Because of that conclusion, he probably would reject (3), a theory based on the belief that dinosaurs were too stupid to survive.

35. **(2)** *Analysis/Nonfiction.* The author does offer descriptions (5) and other information about dinosaurs (4), but his main intent is to argue his position—namely, that those who claim that dinosaurs were stupid just because their brains were relatively small are forgetting an important fact about animal physiology.
36. **(2)** *Literal Comprehension/Poetry.* The quotation marks around each of the four stanzas indicate speech. The first stanza begins with a person addressing "Mother." The second stanza begins with the mother responding to her "baby." That the child is a girl is indicated by the clothing mentioned in the fifth stanza.
37. **(1)** *Literal Comprehension/Poetry.* The mother states that the child cannot go because of the fierce dogs, the clubs and hoses, and the guns that might be fired—all of which could cause the child harm. The mother makes no mention of any of the other choices.
38. **(4)** *Inferential Comprehension/Poetry.* By combining the details of the explosion that was heard (line 25), the frantic search by the mother through the rubble of the church (line 29), and the mother's discovery of only one shoe that her daughter had worn, it can be concluded that the church exploded and her child is dead.
39. **(2)** *Analysis/Poetry.* The dialogue makes the two characters more real than simple description would have. That and the story form involve the reader in the characters' lives. So the mother's final loss has more impact than if the incident had been described otherwise. This technique is more sympathetic and personal than a news report would be (4). It also delays the climax until the very end (5).
40. **(4)** *Application/Poetry.* The last place the mother expected tragedy to occur was at the church, yet that is where the explosion happened and her daughter died. So the mother would not agree with choice (1). She might think that her daughter would have been safer at the Freedom March (2). It is unlikely that the mother would agree with (3) and (5) even though the child might have lived if she had disobeyed and stayed away from the church.
41. **(3)** *Literal Comprehension/Commentary.* The author says this in lines 40–41. Munny says, "it's for the money. But it's really because a man's job is his life."
42. **(3)** *Literal Comprehension/Commentary.* Munny is described as a gunfighter (line 23) who has retired and can't even shoot or ride well (lines 26–27). (1) refers to Eastwood's earlier movie roles. (2) refers to what Munny probably was earlier in life. Munny certainly is not confident and can't quite be described as a hero (5).
43. **(2)** *Inferential Comprehension/Commentary.* The film's difference from earlier Westerns is suggested in two places. First, it is "Eastwood's meditation" (line 19), in which the images of hero and villain blur into each other, unlike the old, clear-cut images of good and bad guys. Second, the movie portrays the Old West as hard and unromantic. The gunfights were not heroic (lines 46–48). The reviewer concludes this observation with the suggestion that the movie is also intended to make the audience think about "death in the movies." All these are in contrast to the casual approach to shoot-em-ups.
44. **(2)** *Analysis/Commentary.* The kid does not appreciate the role Eastwood has played in movie history. The "frame" is intended to remind the reader of his importance. Even though the boy may not be properly impressed, Eastwood has not been forgotten (1).
45. **(1)** *Analysis/Commentary.* A character's own words often reveal more about him than a description would. The reviewer has selected quotations that show how Munny sees his past and what he has become. Rather than use the quotations to introduce ideas (5), the reviewer uses them as examples.